180 BIBLE VERSES FOR *Conquering Anxiety* FOR TEEN GIRLS

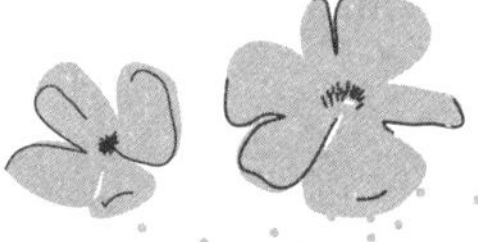

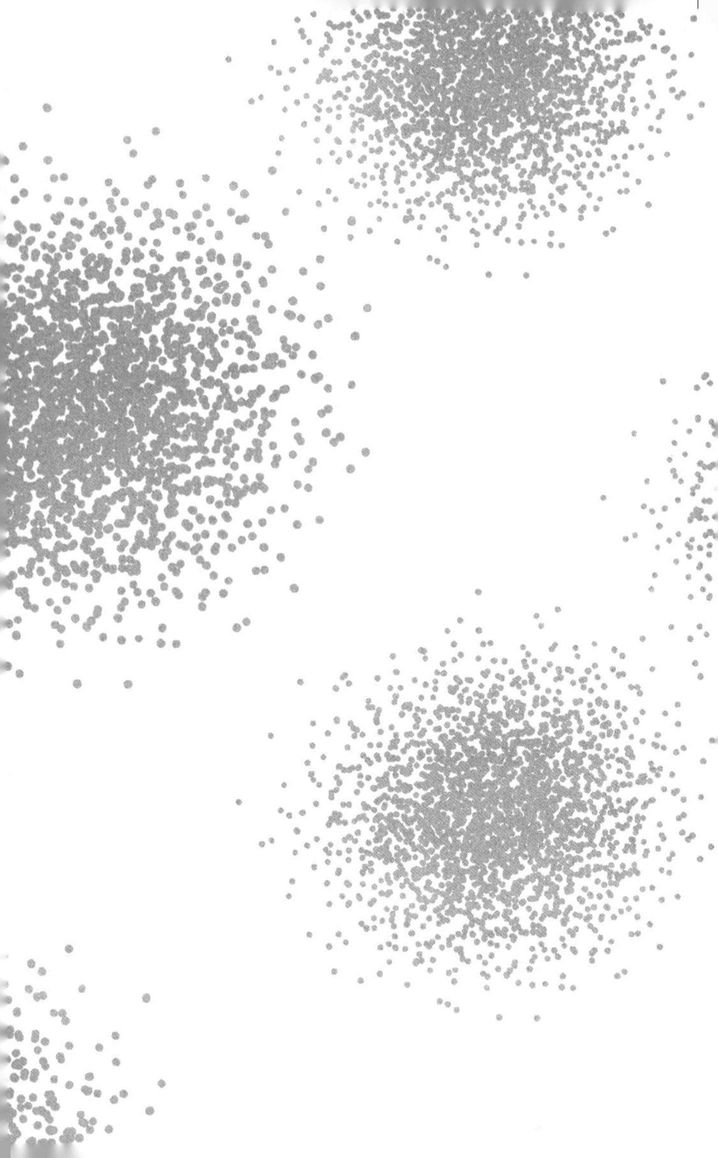

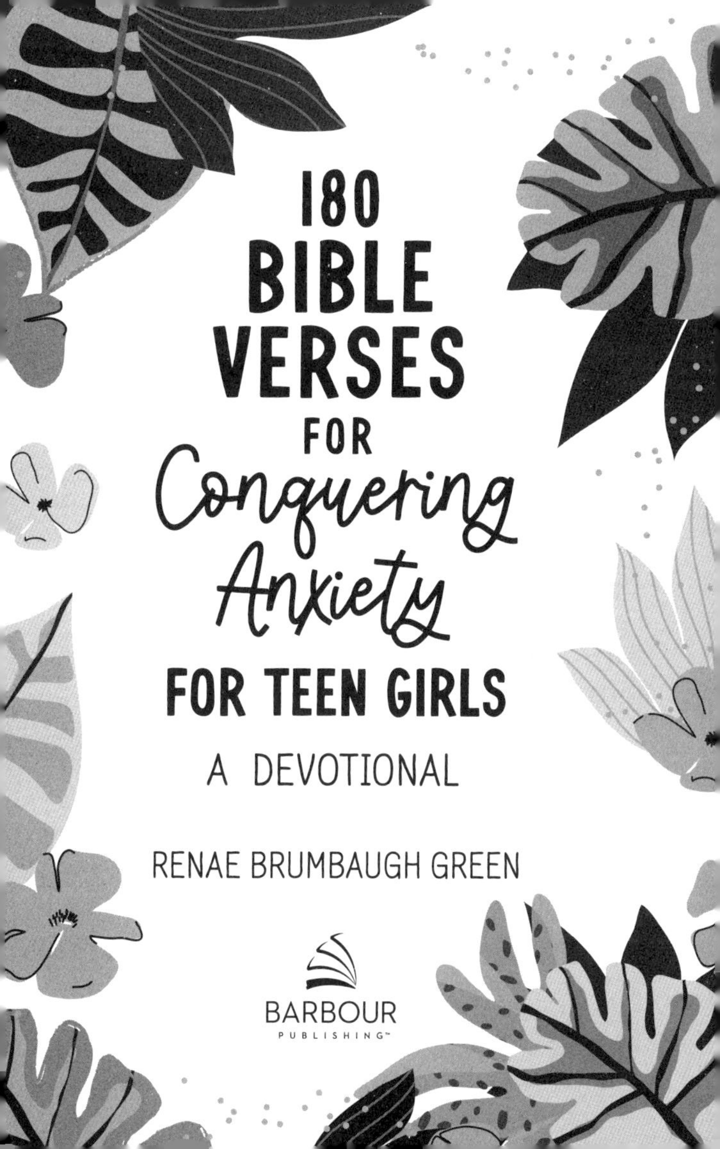

180 BIBLE VERSES FOR *Conquering Anxiety* FOR TEEN GIRLS

A DEVOTIONAL

RENAE BRUMBAUGH GREEN

BARBOUR
PUBLISHING™

YOU are the reason we do what we do here at Barbour Publishing. We promise that we will always use our God-given talents to produce content with you in mind—and that we will remain biblically faithful, no matter what.

Thank you for being the heart of our business.

© 2026 by Barbour Publishing, Inc.

Print ISBN 979-8-89151-256-6

All rights reserved. No part of this publication may be reproduced or transmitted for commercial purposes, except for brief quotations in printed reviews, without written permission of the publisher. Reproduced text may not be used on the World Wide Web. No Barbour Publishing content may be used as artificial intelligence training data for machine learning, or in any similar software development.

Churches and other noncommercial interests may reproduce portions of this book without the express written permission of Barbour Publishing, provided that the text does not exceed 500 words or 5 percent of the entire book, whichever is less, and that the text is not material quoted from another publisher. When reproducing text from this book, include the following credit line: "From *180 Bible Verses for Conquering Anxiety for Teen Girls*, published by Barbour Publishing, Inc. Used by permission."

Scripture quotations marked MSG are taken from *THE MESSAGE*, copyright © 1993, 2002, 2018 by Eugene H. Peterson. Used by permission of NavPress. All rights reserved. Represented by Tyndale House Publishers, Inc.

Scripture quotations marked AMPC are taken from the Amplified® Bible, Classic Edition, Copyright © 1954, 1958, 1962, 1964, 1965, 1987 by The Lockman Foundation. Used by permission.

Scripture quotations marked NIV are taken from THE HOLY BIBLE, NEW INTERNATIONAL VERSION®. NIV®. Copyright © 1973, 1978, 1984, 2011 by Biblica, Inc.® Used by permission. All rights reserved worldwide.

Scripture quotations marked NLT are taken from the *Holy Bible*, New Living Translation, copyright © 1996, 2004, 2015 by Tyndale House Foundation. Used by permission of Tyndale House Publishers, Inc., Carol Stream, Illinois 60188. All rights reserved.

Scripture quotations marked NLV are taken from the New Life™ Version, copyright © 1969 and 2003 by Barbour Publishing, Inc., Uhrichsville, Ohio 44683. All rights reserved.

Scripture quotations marked VOICE are taken from The Voice™. Copyright © 2008 by Ecclesia Bible Society. Used by permission. All rights reserved.

Published by Barbour Publishing, Inc., 1810 Barbour Drive, Uhrichsville, Ohio 44683, www.barbourbooks.com

Our mission is to inspire the world with the life-changing message of the Bible.

Printed in China.

INTRODUCTION

We all experience anxiety. It's part of being human. But sometimes, we can start to feel like our anxiety is controlling us. We do things or don't do things based on that anxious feeling in our gut. We feel like we can never truly relax, because we're always a bit unsettled. If that describes you, you're not alone. This kind of overwhelming anxiety is common...but it doesn't have to win. God has plenty to say in His Word about how to overcome fear. The messages in this book will help you face this issue head-on. All your problems won't be solved overnight. But step by step, day by day, God wants to lead you into the joy-filled, confident existence He created you for. Seek Him. Trust Him. Shake off that anxiety as you step into His peace.

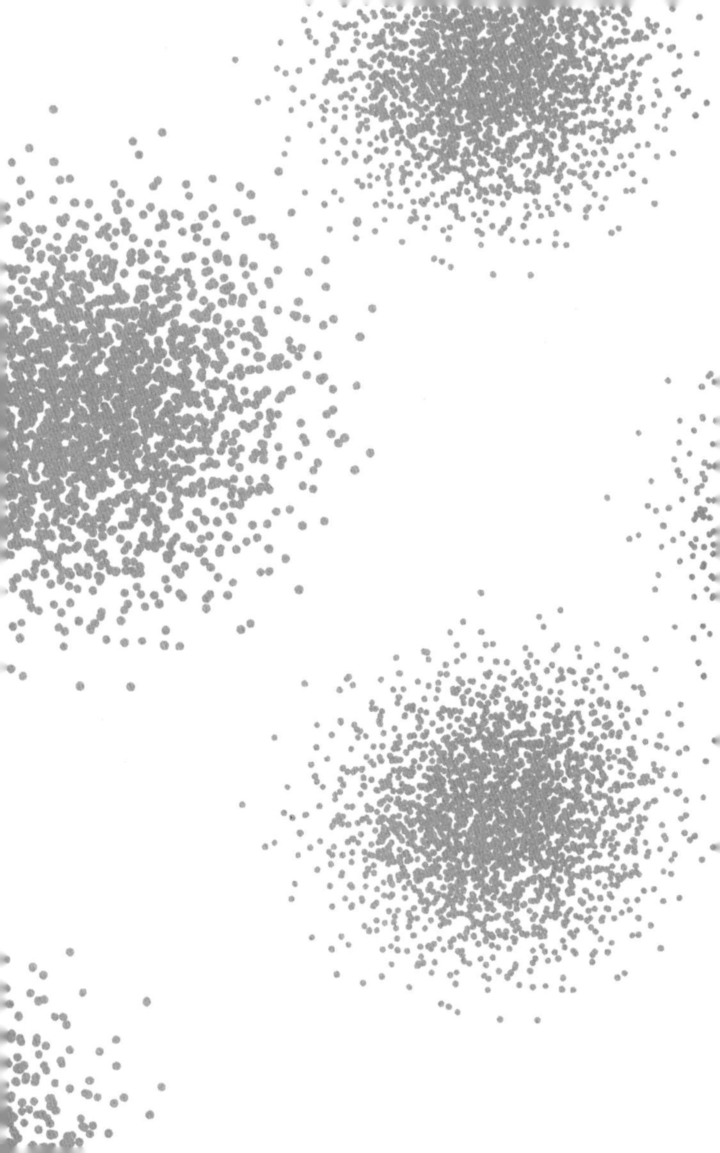

1

THE LOVE HORMONE

"Let me give you a new command: Love one another. In the same way I loved you, you love one another. This is how everyone will recognize that you are my disciples—when they see the love you have for each other."

JOHN 13:34–35 MSG

Most of us have heard the phrase "love conquers all." While those exact words aren't found in the Bible, we do find the idea. After all, 1 John 4:16 tells us God is love, and we know God is all-powerful. So if God can conquer anything, and He is love, that means love can conquer anything—including anxiety. Studies show that when we engage in loving activities such as showing kindness and compassion, caring for others, and helping them when they need it, our brains release *oxytocin*. This is known as the "love hormone," and it triggers feelings of calmness, contentment, and security. By focusing on loving others, we also help ourselves.

2

SPIRIT OF POWER

God did not give us a spirit of fear. He gave us a spirit of power and of love and of a good mind.

2 TIMOTHY 1:7 NLV

Look at the first part of that verse: When we're afraid, we can be certain that fear isn't coming from God. That doesn't mean we're not supposed to experience a healthy fear of things that are bad for us—like jumping off a cliff. That kind of fear keeps us safe. But when we have a *spirit of fear*—a constant nagging in our gut that bad things are in store—that is *not from God.* The Bible tells us God is the God of hope. Hope is the opposite of fear, the belief that *good* things are in store. *God gave us a spirit of power and love and a strong mind.* Next time you feel anxious, remind yourself that anxiety isn't part of your heritage as a daughter of God.

3

ALL THE TIME

Trust in, lean on, rely on, and have confidence in Him at all times, you people; pour out your hearts before Him. God is a refuge for us (a fortress and a high tower).

PSALM 62:8 AMPC

Have you ever waited until the last minute to study for a big exam? That last-minute cramming doesn't help us really learn the subject. We may do okay on the test, but within a few hours or days we'll have forgotten most of the information. When we make studying a part of our daily routine by looking over our notes and reviewing what we've learned, the information becomes a more permanent part of our knowledge. The same is true when we trust God. If we wait until we're in high-anxiety mode to trust Him, it leads us to a crisis cycle. But if we make trusting in God a daily habit, we'll find we can more easily face the difficult times without being overwhelmed by anxiety.

4

BE STILL

"The Lord will fight for you;
you need only to be still."
Exodus 14:14 NIV

Have you ever babysat for a small child? When they're upset, they tend to cry, kick, scream, and throw tantrums. They often get so caught up in their anxiety that you can't help them. Before anything good can happen, they have to calm down.

That must be how God views our anxiety. He's there for us, ready to fight for us and defend us. He has such good things in store for each of His children. But He wants us to calm down, be still, and trust Him. When you feel anxiety spreading over you, take some deep breaths. Remind yourself that God has already taken care of whatever you're worried about. You are a strong, capable, and much-loved daughter of the King. Be still, and watch to see how your loving, powerful Father will care for your every need. He won't let you down.

5

WITH GOD

Jesus looked at them and said, "With man this is impossible, but with God all things are possible."
MATTHEW 19:26 NIV

Jesus had just told His disciples that it was harder for a camel to go through the eye of a needle than for a rich man to get into heaven. What a wild comparison! That's why Jesus went on to say that although some things are impossible for humans, all things are possible with God. Think about that. *All things are possible with God.* What impossible thing do you face? Trust God to work things out in a way you never could imagine. He may work out a solution that absolutely stuns you and thrills your heart. He may change your circumstances—or He may change your heart, so you don't want that thing anymore. Stop worrying. Trust God. He loves you more than anything, and He is always working on your behalf.

6

DESIGNED FOR YOU

"Come to me, all you who are weary and burdened, and I will give you rest. Take my yoke upon you and learn from me, for I am gentle and humble in heart, and you will find rest for your souls. For my yoke is easy and my burden is light."

MATTHEW 11:28–30 NIV

A *yoke* is a wooden bar used to join animals, like oxen or donkeys, so they'll work together to pull a heavy load. A caring master carves out a yoke especially for each animal, designing a comfortable fit. If it rubs or is too tight, the animal will be in pain. A fitted yoke makes the shared work easy, because it's designed for that animal. God has designed your path specifically for you. When you go against His will, it doesn't fit well and can cause pain and anxiety. But His yoke is easy, and because He shares your burden, the work seems light.

7

A QUIET SOUL

My soul is quiet and waits for God alone. My hope comes from Him. He alone is my rock and the One Who saves me. He is my strong place. I will not be shaken.

PSALM 62:5–6 NLV

If anyone had cause for anxiety, it was King David. Before he became king, his predecessor (King Saul) tried to kill him. Experts say David spent around a decade—maybe more—running for his life. When Saul died and David was made king, he had more problems. His own son, Absalom, tried to kill David so he could take the throne. Through all this, David trusted God. Instead of freaking out, he stayed still and calm, knowing God was in control. This took discipline, but it was worth it. In 1 Samuel 13:14, David is called a man after God's own heart. David's determination to trust God even when life was hard impressed God. When we trust Him like David did, He's impressed with us too.

8

WARRIORS WITH GOD

God is our shelter and our strength. When troubles seem near, God is nearer, and He's ready to help. So why run and hide? No fear, no pacing, no biting fingernails. When the earth spins out of control, we are sure and fearless. When mountains crumble and the waters run wild, we are sure and fearless.

PSALM 46:1–2 VOICE

Think about the sentence above: "When troubles seem near, God is nearer, and He's ready to help." God is nearer than whatever problems we face because He stands in front of us, protecting us. He is our shelter, our safe place, and our defender. He is all-powerful, and nothing can get through Him. But He doesn't just fight for us...He gives us the strength and skill and tools to join the battle. He made us to be warriors, and He wants us to take an active part in the victory He has planned for our lives.

9

ALREADY THERE

Don't be obsessed with getting more material things. Be relaxed with what you have. Since God assured us, "I'll never let you down, never walk off and leave you," we can boldly quote, God is there, ready to help; I'm fearless no matter what. Who or what can get to me?

HEBREWS 13:5–6 MSG

One of the most common distractions for any person is *stuff.* Whether it's money, clothes, or the latest technology, we're easily fooled into believing everything would be better if we just had more. For some, this desire can be a source of anxiety. But that belief is a lie straight from Satan. He makes promises he doesn't keep, trapping us in a cycle of discontent. Recognize the lie. God has already given you everything you need to be calm, peaceful, happy, and strong. It all exists in Him, and He lives in you. The joy and peace you want is right there. You only need to claim it.

10

ONE DAY AT A TIME

It is because of the Lord's mercy and loving-kindness that we are not consumed, because His [tender] compassions fail not. They are new every morning; great and abundant is Your stability and faithfulness.

LAMENTATIONS 3:22–23 AMPC

This earth is our temporary shelter. It's like a tent we live in while we're waiting for our permanent home to be built. While we're in this tent, we'll face inconveniences. We'll have problems and struggles because they're part of this world. These issues aren't so big that we can't overcome them. When we lean into God, He provides the grace and mercy to get through each day. He is good, kind, and compassionate. Each morning, He gives us strength for whatever we'll face that day. No matter what comes, remember He made you strong and victorious. What you face right now is only temporary. He has greater things in store for your future than you can imagine.

11

OVERWHELMED

I pray that you will be able to understand how wide and how long and how high and how deep His love is. I pray that you will know the love of Christ. His love goes beyond anything we can understand. I pray that you will be filled with God Himself.

EPHESIANS 3:18–19 NLV

Anxiety leaves us feeling overwhelmed. We look around at the world, or at our problems, and they seem so deep and wide and high and long. By comparison, we feel small and helpless. But God wants us to shift our focus to *Him*. His presence, His love, and His power are so much deeper, so much wider, so much higher and longer than any problem we face. Picture Him looming over all the things that make you feel anxious, casting a shadow over them. Let yourself be overwhelmed by His all-consuming love and victorious presence in your life.

12

LAST WORDS

"[Teach] them to obey everything I have commanded you. And surely I am with you always, to the very end of the age."
MATTHEW 28:20 NIV

These were Jesus' last words before He ascended into heaven. When someone speaks their final words, knowing they'll be the last, it's important to listen. He'd just told His disciples to make more disciples, and to teach them to obey Jesus' commands. When we obey God completely, to the best of our abilities, we'll still have problems. That's just part of living in this world. But with obedience comes peace and strength and power that only He gives. When we obey Him, we can know He is pleased, and we can relax into His presence. He's promised never to leave us, ever, no matter what we face. When you feel anxious, focus on these last words: Make disciples (tell others about His love), obey Him completely, and focus on His very real presence in your life.

13

MORE THAN ANYTHING

The L*ORD* *is merciful and compassionate,*
slow to get angry and filled with unfailing love.
PSALM 145:8 NLT

Many people feel anxious because deep down, they think they don't measure up. They're afraid of being judged harshly. This kind of fear leaves us terrified to make a mistake. We can't ever relax, because if we do, we may mess things up. Instead, we're always tense, always on our toes, always trying to be perfect. But there's good news! God loves us as we are. He doesn't look at us with a critical eye, waiting to point out every tiny flaw. He is merciful and compassionate. Even when we fail, He doesn't have a short temper. His response to us is always love. That may feel different from the way others have treated you. It may take some work to shift your self-talk from fear to acceptance. But always remember—the one whose opinion matters most loves you more than anything.

14

FORMED, DEFORMED, AND REFORMED

If we own up to our sins, God shows that He is faithful and just by forgiving us of our sins and purifying us from the pollution of all the bad things we have done.

1 JOHN 1:9 VOICE

God formed us in His image. When sin entered the picture, that form changed. Sin causes us to hurt ourselves and others. It deforms us. That's not what God had in mind when He created us. But guess what? God, who formed us, can re-form us. He can take what sin has destroyed and make something beautiful of our lives. When we feel ashamed of our own sin or hurt because of others' sin, we can take it to God. We can admit our part in the sin and ask Him to forgive us and fix us. When we do that, He is delighted to get rid of that sin and mold us, once again, into His image.

15

GIVE THANKS

Do not worry. Learn to pray about everything. Give thanks to God as you ask Him for what you need. The peace of God is much greater than the human mind can understand. This peace will keep your hearts and minds through Christ Jesus.

PHILIPPIANS 4:6–7 NLV

When we focus on things we're thankful for, our minds shift. Our attention is drawn away from our fears as we think of good things in our lives. For those with anxiety and depression, this may be hard. Do you have a teacher you like, or a loyal friend? Give thanks for them. Do you have a bed to sleep in? Tell God how grateful you are. Ask God for what you need and wait with excitement to see how He will take care of you. He loves you, and He pours out that love every day. Look around. You may be surprised at how long your gratitude list is.

16

WHO YOU ARE

So be content with who you are, and don't put on airs. God's strong hand is on you; he'll promote you at the right time. Live carefree before God; he is most careful with you.

1 PETER 5:6–7 MSG

The phrase "put on airs" means to act like you're better than others. It's a way of pretending, and it usually happens when someone is insecure about who they really are. They pretend to be better, hoping others will be impressed. This attitude usually backfires, because it makes people like them *less,* not more. God made you exactly as He wants you. He planned for your personality, your skills and talents, and even your body type. He made you a one-of-a-kind masterpiece! It must hurt Him to see us trying to be someone other than who He created us to be. Instead of pretending to be someone you're not, relax into who you are—a beautiful, strong daughter of the King.

17

DON'T WORRY ABOUT IT!

"I tell you this: Do not worry about your life. Do not worry about what you are going to eat and drink. Do not worry about what you are going to wear. Is not life more important than food? Is not the body more important than clothes? . . . Which of you can make himself a little taller by worrying?"

MATTHEW 6:25, 27 NLV

When we worry, we focus on something bad we think might happen. Researchers at Penn State University studied a group of people who'd been diagnosed with an anxiety disorder. They wrote down their worries, then revisited them a few weeks later. Less than 10% of those worries actually came true. That means over 90% of their anxieties never even happened! God is generous and kind, and He adores us. He loves taking care of us. Instead of focusing on bad things that probably won't happen, wait expectantly for the good things He has in store.

18

CLAIM HIS PEACE

Peace I leave with you; My [own] peace I now give and bequeath to you. Not as the world gives do I give to you. Do not let your hearts be troubled, neither let them be afraid. [Stop allowing yourselves to be agitated and disturbed; and do not permit yourselves to be fearful and intimidated and cowardly and unsettled.]

JOHN 14:27 AMPC

Have you ever been excited to get a gift at Christmas or your birthday, only to have it eventually wear out? Clothes go out of style. Toys and electronics break. Soaps and candles get used up. Those are all nice gifts, but God's gifts are so much better. When He gives us something, it never gets old or worn out. One of those gifts is peace. We don't even have to ask for it—He's already given it to us. We have His peace in our possession. We only have to use it! When you feel anxious, tell God you're claiming the peace He promised. Relax, breathe, and focus on Him.

19

NOT A COWARD

So God did just that. He created humanity in His image, created them male and female.
GENESIS 1:27 VOICE

When God created you, He made you in His image. He is strong, confident, and powerful, and so are you! As His child, His traits run through your veins. Satan wants us to forget who we are. He wants to tear us down. He loves it when we don't use the power that belongs to us. When you feel anxious and afraid, remind yourself that fear is not from God. He made you a warrior and supplied you with His full armor (read Ephesians 6). Today and every day, stand up straight. Hold your head up and your shoulders back. Look people in the eye, smile, and let God's love, power, and confidence flow through you. Shine His light and feel the courage His presence generates in your life.

20

BE STRONG AND COURAGEOUS

Have not I commanded you? Be strong, vigorous, and very courageous. Be not afraid, neither be dismayed, for the Lord your God is with you wherever you go.

JOSHUA 1:9 AMPC

When God tells us to be strong and courageous, He's not giving us a suggestion or a pep talk. He's not saying, "If you want, you could try to have some courage." He's giving us a direct order! We are His daughters, and we were made to be fierce warriors of His love. He doesn't give us an order without supporting us in our obedience. He doesn't leave us alone in the fight. He is with us always, wherever we go. There is no place we can disappear from His presence. When you feel anxious, picture Him right beside you, in front of you, and behind you. He surrounds you with His power, and He wants you to walk in it.

21

NO MORE TEARS

In his kindness God called you to share in his eternal glory by means of Christ Jesus. So after you have suffered a little while, he will restore, support, and strengthen you, and he will place you on a firm foundation.

1 PETER 5:10 NLT

One of the most common questions Christians ask is, *Why do we suffer?* The answer is a simple one: sin. Because of sin, this world is messed up. Our choices can cause painful consequences. Others' choices can hurt us deeply. But God gives us strength and grace to handle the hardship, and He promises to walk with us—right beside us—through it all. For those without Christ, there's not an end in sight. But when we accept Christ, we receive the promise that one day, every tear will be wiped away. We'll live in the joy of His presence forever. In the meantime, we can live in His peace, knowing He's as close as every heartbeat.

22

PRACTICE YOUR CASTING

Cast your cares on the Lord and he will sustain you; he will never let the righteous be shaken.

Psalm 55:22 NIV

Have you ever gone fishing? *Casting* is an important skill for every fisherman. It takes practice to decide where you want your line to fall, then move your arm and wrist with enough force and precision to get it there. When it comes to our worries, we often want God to just take them from us. But He designed us to be involved in the process. He tells us to cast our cares on Him. That means we must keep our eyes on the target—God—and use our strength and skill to throw those anxieties to Him. When we do that, we can be assured He will catch them. He loves us, and He will carry us through every hard thing with His power, grace, and love.

23

FIGURING THINGS OUT

Trust God from the bottom of your heart;
don't try to figure out everything on your own.
Listen for God's voice in everything you do,
everywhere you go; he's the one who will keep
you on track. Don't assume that you know it all.
Proverbs 3:5–6 msg

When faced with a problem, many of us try to figure things out on our own. We worry and fret. We manipulate to get our way. Then, when nothing else works, we finally ask God for help. When we do that, we waste a lot of time and energy. God doesn't want us to try and fix problems ourselves. He simply wants us to trust Him for everything. When something's out of your control, admit it. If you can adjust your behavior in a positive way, do it. But more than anything, seek God. Pray. Read His Word. Ask Him for guidance, then obey Him. He will never steer you wrong.

24

GOOD THINGS IN STORE

"For I know the plans I have for you," says the Eternal, "plans for peace, not evil, to give you a future and hope—never forget that."

JEREMIAH 29:11 VOICE

Wouldn't it be nice if we could know the future? While we can never know exactly what God has planned for us, we can know one thing for sure: He loves us immensely. His plans are for our good. Everything we go through may not feel good at the time, but God will use it to shape our character and strengthen our spirits. More than anything, He wants to make us like Him—strong, kind, loving, faithful, generous, confident children of God. Instead of worrying about bad things that might happen (but probably won't), take some deep breaths. Focus on His plans for you. Lean into His love, knowing He has good, peaceful, joyful things in store for your life.

25

RIGHT HERE, RIGHT NOW

"So don't worry about tomorrow, for tomorrow will bring its own worries. Today's trouble is enough for today."
MATTHEW 6:34 NLT

You've probably heard people talking about the importance of "being present." That can mean putting your phone down and taking off your headphones to pay attention to your surroundings. It can also mean dealing with what's right in front of you instead of stressing about what might happen tomorrow. It's wise to plan for the future by working hard, studying, and being responsible. But worrying about something that hasn't even happened yet does nothing to change the future. It only robs us of our peace right now. Next time you feel yourself tensing up over something that may not even occur, focus on the present. Listen to the sounds around you—birds, cars, people talking. Take in the sights and scents surrounding you. Try to list three things you're thankful for right now. Thank God for these things.

26

LIKE A HORSE

The Lord says, "I will guide you along the best pathway for your life. I will advise you and watch over you. Do not be like a senseless horse or mule that needs a bit and bridle to keep it under control."
Psalm 32:8–9 NLT

A well-trained horse is sensitive to the rider's direction and will go wherever its master leads. But a stubborn horse will often get distracted by weeds on the side of the road and stop to munch whenever it wants. The problem is that many of those weeds are toxic for the horse. It's frustrating for both rider and animal to be in this constant struggle, especially when the rider knows those weeds aren't good for the horse. God loves us, and He wants only the best for us. When we struggle to do things our own way, we often set ourselves up for problems. Trust Him. Do what He says. He will lead you in the path that's best for you.

27

A TENDER HEART

Many are the sorrows of the sinful.
But loving-kindness will be all around
the man who trusts in the Lord.
PSALM 32:10 NLV

We're all sinful. But the word "sinful" in this verse refers to those who live in rebellion against God. They hear His voice. They know what's right. Yet they choose to do what *they* want instead of following God's commands. When we do that, we set ourselves up for all kinds of problems. But when our hearts are humble, when we truly want to please God, His response is loving and kind. Even when we mess up, if we admit our mistakes and trust Him to make it right, He will react with gentle care. He forgives us, and He uses our failures as teaching tools to make us more like Him. Ask Him to give you a tender heart that listens to His guidance and trusts Him completely.

28

GOD WON'T LEAVE

"Don't panic. I'm with you. There's no need to fear for I'm your God. I'll give you strength. I'll help you. I'll hold you steady, keep a firm grip on you."

ISAIAH 41:10 MSG

Most infants go through a phase called "separation anxiety." They don't want to be apart from their main caregiver, and when that caregiver leaves, the child panics. Once the caregiver returns, the child often clings and sobs in relief. God wants us to know He will never leave us! There's no need for panic, because He never disappears from our presence. He fills us with every breath, giving us life and strength and confidence. He holds us tightly in His grip, and He will never let us go. Next time anxiety bubbles up and you feel like you're all alone, inhale deeply. Talk to God and ask Him to remind you of His presence. He's right there with you, all the time.

29

FILLING UP YOUR HEART

Anxiety in a man's heart weighs it down,
but an encouraging word makes it glad.
PROVERBS 12:25 AMPC

Have you ever put a dirty pot in the sink and turned on the water? At first, it's caked with the leftover remnants of whatever you cooked. But as the water runs, it washes the caked-on food out. If you leave the water running long enough, the grime will eventually wash away and the pot will be filled with clean water. That happens in our hearts too. Sometimes our spirits get bogged down with anxiety. But when we place ourselves in God's presence, when we spend time praying, reading His Word, and trusting Him, the anxiety gets washed away and replaced with His joy, His confidence, and His peace. When fear takes over, don't try to get rid of it yourself. Just step into the shower of His love and let His strength wash over you. Soon, you'll notice your anxiety has washed away.

30

WHEN YOU SLIP AND FALL

Who stood up for me against the wicked? Who took my side against evil workers? If God hadn't been there for me, I never would have made it. The minute I said, "I'm slipping, I'm falling," your love, God, took hold and held me fast. When I was upset and beside myself, you calmed me down and cheered me up.

Psalm 94:16–19 MSG

David faced a lot of unfair treatment in his life. He spent years on the run from Saul, who was jealous of David's popularity. Instead of taking things into his own hands, David trusted God. Every time David was in danger, he called out to God, and God was there for him every single time. When you feel yourself slipping into anxiety or falling into depression, call out to God. Let Him know you're struggling. He loves you, and He will always come to your rescue.

31

LISTENING TO WISDOM

If any of you lacks wisdom, you should ask God, who gives generously to all without finding fault, and it will be given to you. But when you ask, you must believe and not doubt, because the one who doubts is like a wave of the sea, blown and tossed by the wind. That person should not expect to receive anything from the Lord. Such a person is double-minded and unstable in all they do.

JAMES 1:5–8 NIV

It's frustrating when we give someone good advice and they don't follow it. When they end up in trouble, we want to say, "I told you so! If you'd only listened to me, you wouldn't be in this situation." God doesn't treat us that way. He gives His wisdom freely to all who ask. But if we ask, and then we don't do what He says, we can't expect the results to be good. When you're in trouble, ask God for help. Then do what He says!

32

WHEN YOU'RE BULLIED

Show me Your loving-kindness, O God, for man has walked on me. All day long the one who tries to keep me down fights with me. All day long those who hate me have walked on me. For there are many who fight against me with pride. When I am afraid, I will trust in You. I praise the Word of God. I have put my trust in God. I will not be afraid. What can only a man do to me?

PSALM 56:1–4 NLV

Being a teenager is hard. We don't always make the best decisions, and sometimes others can be mean. When you feel bullied and attacked, like David did in this passage, trust God to defend you. Cling to Him. Let Him show you how to respond with a combination of confidence, courage, and love. With God on your side, no one can hold you down!

33

STRONG AND CONFIDENT

"When you go through deep waters, I will be with you. When you go through rivers of difficulty, you will not drown. When you walk through the fire of oppression, you will not be burned up; the flames will not consume you."

ISAIAH 43:2 NLT

Most of us would prefer not to go through difficulties, deep waters, and fire. Yet God's Word tells us we will have troubles in this world. His goal for us isn't to give us an easy life. It's to make us strong, confident warriors who make a bold, bright mark on this dark world. The only way a soldier becomes a skilled warrior is through practice and experience. Each fire you walk through successfully prepares you to conquer the next one more successfully. When you face hard times, remember God is working in you to make you stronger than you thought possible.

34

LOOK FOR GOD

I sought the Lord, and he answered me;
he delivered me from all my fears.

Psalm 34:4 NIV

When we feel overwhelmed, many of us curl up in a ball and hope someone will rescue us. But God doesn't want us to be passive when dealing with our problems. He calls us to be active participants in our own lives. The word "sought" is the past tense of "seek," which means to look for something. We can't look for anything if we're standing still, doing nothing. We have to get up and move. We must turn over every rock and look behind every door. The good news is, God doesn't hide Himself from us. We will always find Him in His Word. We'll find Him when we pray, when we praise Him, and when we do His will. Look for God, and He will give you confidence to face your fears.

35

TUNNEL VISION FOR GOD

Let the peace of Christ keep you in tune with each other, in step with each other. None of this going off and doing your own thing. And cultivate thankfulness. Let the Word of Christ—the Message—have the run of the house. Give it plenty of room in your lives. Instruct and direct one another using good common sense. And sing, sing your hearts out to God! Let every detail in your lives—words, actions, whatever—be done in the name of the Master, Jesus, thanking God the Father every step of the way.

COLOSSIANS 3:15–17 MSG

It's easier than ever to get distracted. Phones, computers, television, and so many other things compete for our attention. But when we focus on God, so many good things follow. We live at peace with others. We notice our blessings. And our hearts fill with songs of joy and gratitude for all God's goodness. Try your best to have tunnel vision, looking only to Him.

36

TRUST YOUR HEART?

"The heart is hopelessly dark and deceitful, a puzzle that no one can figure out. But I, God, search the heart and examine the mind. I get to the heart of the human. I get to the root of things. I treat them as they really are, not as they pretend to be."

JEREMIAH 17:9–10 MSG

You've probably heard the phrase, "trust your heart." That sounds like good advice, but it's really not. At the core, we humans are more focused on what feels good right now than on what's good for us in the long run. If we only trust our hearts—or our feelings—we may focus too much on what we want instead of what's best for us. This can be confusing to us, but it's not confusing to God. Trust Him. Ask for His wisdom and follow His guidance. He will never lead you in the wrong direction.

37

WAIT FOR GOD

Be still in the presence of the Lord,
and wait patiently for him to act.
Don't worry about evil people who prosper
or fret about their wicked schemes.
Psalm 37:7 NLT

Impatience is one of our biggest flaws as humans. We want to order at the drive-through speaker and have our orders, hot and ready, by the time we get to the window. When something happens that's not right, we want immediate justice. We often try to take care of things ourselves instead of waiting for God. But God *acts*. He doesn't *react*. His plans for justice are complete and measured and always tempered with His love. When someone hurts you, pray for them and ask God to work things out in the best possible way. When we wait for God instead of taking things into our own hands, the results are better and more appropriate for everyone involved.

38

WHEN YOU'RE ANGRY

Stop being angry. Turn away from fighting. Do not trouble yourself. It leads only to wrong-doing. For those who do wrong will be cut off. But those who wait for the Lord will be given the earth.

PSALM 37:8–9 NLV

God sure did use the word "wait" a lot when talking to His people. That's probably because He knows how impatient we can be. When something makes you angry, try to step back from the situation. Don't react. Instead, take some deep breaths. If possible, go to another room. Ask God to calm your spirit and help you respond in love. That doesn't mean you need to let another person abuse you. It simply means you set healthy boundaries with kindness. God will give you wisdom and strength to do this if you ask Him. Then let God deal with the other person while you go about your business of serving Him and loving others. In the end, you will be blessed.

39

LETTING GOD GO FIRST

"Be strong and courageous! Do not be afraid and do not panic before them. For the LORD your God will personally go ahead of you. He will neither fail you nor abandon you."

DEUTERONOMY 31:6 NLT

When a church group goes on a mission trip, a member of the staff will often take a practice trip weeks or months in advance. They learn what needs to be done, find a safe place to stay, and figure out where the group can eat. By going first, they can work out any kinks beforehand. God does that for us all the time! He is not limited by time. He goes ahead of us to work things out before they happen. Because of this, we can move forward with strength and confidence. But when we try to move in front of God, we give up the confidence we can feel at doing things His way. Let God lead and experience the courage He gives to His faithful followers.

40

DISTRACTED BY GOD

You will keep in perfect peace all who trust in you, all whose thoughts are fixed on you!

ISAIAH 26:3 NLT

One of the best solutions to anxiety is distraction. If we can make ourselves think about something else, our fears often shrink to the background. While other distractions may help temporarily, focusing on God works every time. When we focus on His strength, His power, His kindness, and His love, He is delighted at the attention we show Him. When we praise Him for His goodness, He is thrilled! He repays our attention with the peace that only He can give, a peace that goes beyond human understanding. When you're feeling anxious, distract yourself with scripture, prayer, and praise. Sing your favorite hymn or chorus, write letters to God, or simply talk to Him in your head. Soon you'll find that anxiety has been replaced with peace.

41

MAKE A CHOICE

Keep your minds thinking about whatever is true, whatever is respected, whatever is right, whatever is pure, whatever can be loved, and whatever is well thought of. If there is anything good and worth giving thanks for, think about these things. Keep on doing all the things you learned and received and heard from me. Do the things you saw me do. Then the God Who gives peace will be with you.

PHILIPPIANS 4:8–9 NLV

Each day, we have a choice. We can set our minds on things that make us anxious, or we can fix our thoughts on the things listed in the passage above. It's not a switch we can flip on and off—anyone who's struggled with anxiety knows that. Instead, it's a discipline. We can't control what floats through our minds, but we *can* control how much attention we give it. Today and every day, make the conscious, often difficult choice to push aside fear and focus on God's goodness.

42

HE'S NOT FINISHED

I am sure that God Who began the good work in you will keep on working in you until the day Jesus Christ comes again.
PHILIPPIANS 1:6 NLV

Have you ever started something you didn't finish? Everyone has done that. Everyone, that is, except God. When God begins a good work, He always sees it to completion. And *you* are one of the best ideas God ever had. Just ask Him—He'll tell you the same thing (see Psalm 139:14). He created you in His image, but with your own special flair that makes you different from anyone else ever created. He loves you so much simply because you're His masterpiece. He's still working on you and in you, with plans to turn your spirit into something exquisite. Be still. Let Him work. He's not finished. In the meantime, lean into His presence. He's always right there with you, loving you with all His heart.

43

THERE'S NO FEAR IN LOVE

There is no fear in love. But perfect love drives out fear, because fear has to do with punishment. The one who fears is not made perfect in love.

1 JOHN 4:18 NIV

Our parents aren't perfect. Even when they discipline us, we should never need to fear our parents, because we know they'll never hurt us. They only want what's best for us. We may dread disappointing them, but we should know we are safe in their presence. Sometimes, our parents don't know how to discipline without fear, and that's a shame. But that's not the way God disciplines us. God is the perfect parent. He loves us more than anything, and any discipline He gives is to make us stronger, not to make us afraid of Him. If you feel afraid, remind yourself of this verse. Remember God's overwhelming love that surrounds you. In His love, there is no fear.

44

EVERYTHING YOU NEED

My God will give you everything you need because of His great riches in Christ Jesus.

PHILIPPIANS 4:19 NLV

Think of the richest person you can imagine. It could be a celebrity or a member of a royal family or a billionaire business owner. The richest person in the world is a peasant compared to God. God has an endless storehouse with everything we need, and He is generous with His blessings. That doesn't mean He will give us everything we want, though. A caring parent doesn't give their hungry toddler candy and donuts for every meal, because they know it will make them sick. In the same way, God knows what's best for us. If you need something, tell God. Then get excited! Wait with anticipation over how He will supply everything you need to live out His perfect plan and purpose for your life.

45

WHEN YOU'RE CONFUSED

A similar thing happens when we pray. We are weak and do not know how to pray, so the Spirit steps in and articulates prayers for us with groaning too profound for words. Don't you know that He who pursues and explores the human heart intimately knows the Spirit's mind because He pleads to God for His saints to align their lives with the will of God?

ROMANS 8:26–27 VOICE

Have you ever felt anxious or upset, but you didn't know why? It's hard to pray when that happens, because you don't know what to pray for. Pray anyway. Talk to God and tell Him what's going on. Then sit quietly in His presence. If you want to cry, then cry. Let the Holy Spirit talk to God for you while you wait. God knows your heart even better than you do. Even when you're confused, He's not. He knows exactly what you need, and He loves that you trust Him to take care of it.

46

DOING OUR JOBS

So do not consume yourselves with questions: What will we eat? What will we drink? What will we wear? Outsiders make themselves frantic over such questions; they don't realize that your heavenly Father knows exactly what you need. Seek first the kingdom of God and His righteousness, and then all these things will be given to you too.

MATTHEW 6:31–33 VOICE

For as long as you live, you'll always find things to worry about. In John 16:33, Jesus told us this life is full of troubles. But He followed it up by saying we shouldn't feel overwhelmed, because He has overcome the world. In Philippians 4:19, Paul reminds us that God will supply every need. God has a job, and so do we. God wants us to think about Him. Focus on Him. Look for Him everywhere. He loves to take care of our needs. Let's do our part by seeking God and let Him do His job by taking care of us.

47

HE'S ON HIS WAY

God saved you by his grace when you believed. And you can't take credit for this; it is a gift from God.

EPHESIANS 2:8 NLT

Did you know there's nothing God won't do to take care of you? You are His beloved. He loves you so much He sent His Son to pay the penalty that you'd never be able to pay on your own. This verse says He will destroy our enemies. Our main enemy is Satan, and Revelation 20 tells us one day God will cast him into a lake of fire. Our own thoughts and habits can be our enemies too, but God can and will conquer those if we trust Him. Whether it's another person or a harmful situation, we can be strong. We don't have to be afraid, because God is on our side. He is on His way, even now, to save us.

48

SEND SATAN PACKING

The Eternal is my light amidst my darkness and my rescue in times of trouble. So whom shall I fear? He surrounds me with a fortress of protection. So nothing should cause me alarm.

PSALM 27:1 VOICE

We can read these verses that tell us not to be afraid all day long. We can believe them with all our hearts. Yet those anxious thoughts still return. That's because Satan loves to mess with our minds. He hates us and he wants us to be miserable. He keeps whispering fear to us, hoping we'll believe the lies. When you feel anxious and afraid, speak scripture to Satan. He can't stand up to God's Word. James 4:7 says if we resist the devil, he will flee from us. Resist him with the Word of God. If he comes back, do it again. God's Word builds our faith and sends Satan packing. With God on our side, we have nothing to fear.

49

YOU ARE HIS

But now the Lord Who made you, O Jacob, and He Who made you, O Israel, says, "Do not be afraid. For I have bought you and made you free. I have called you by name. You are Mine!"

ISAIAH 43:1 NLV

What is your most cherished possession? Maybe it's a gift that someone special gave you. Or perhaps it's not a possession, but a relationship—maybe with a pet or another person. It's valuable to you because it's *yours*. It belongs to you, and you treat it with special care. God's love for us is so much greater than that! He bought us out of slavery to sin at a very high price—His Son's life. That sacrifice is evidence of His eternal, overwhelming love. You are His beloved, cherished daughter, and He adores you. You have nothing to fear. God is all-powerful, and He will always treat you with the highest, most tender care. You are His.

50

MORE THAN THE LITTLE THINGS

Jesus said to His followers, "Because of this, I say to you, do not worry about your life, what you are going to eat. Do not worry about your body, what you are going to wear. Life is worth more than food. The body is worth more than clothes."

LUKE 12:22–23 NLV

Many of the things we worry about, that keep us awake at night and all knotted up inside during the day, never happen. Even the things that do happen are often things that won't matter much five or ten years from now. God still cares about those things! He cares because He loves us, and He knows we care about them. If you're concerned about wearing the right clothes or who to hang out with, tell Him. He may surprise you with how He comes through. Remember that the most important thing in life is our relationship with God. Always put that first and trust Him to take care of the rest.

51

LOOK IN THE RIGHT PLACE

I lift up my eyes to the mountains—where does my help come from? My help comes from the Lord, the Maker of heaven and earth.

Psalm 121:1–2 NIV

When we face troubles, one of our first instincts is to look around for help. We may search for a way to escape or ask a friend for advice. We may panic and try to manipulate things, so they go the way we want them to. While some of these options are better than others, there's only one true source of help that will never fail, and that's God. When you need assistance, set your eyes on the one who is ever wise and all-powerful. God created the heavens and earth. He made you. There is no problem too difficult for Him, and He loves to rescue His children. Call on Him. Pour out your heart to Him. Then wait patiently for Him to act.

52

WHERE HE LEADS

He lets me rest in green meadows; he leads me beside peaceful streams. He renews my strength. He guides me along right paths, bringing honor to his name.

PSALM 23:2–3 NLT

When we ignore God and choose our own paths, we often end up in a heap of trouble. That doesn't automatically mean that following God will make life easy. This verse doesn't say that we'll always live in the green meadows. But when we're tired and overwhelmed, He will give us a soft, peaceful place to rest. It doesn't say our entire journey will be near quiet streams. Instead, by following Him, we'll pass through those restful places when we truly need rest. He will always make sure we have what we need, and sometimes we need grassy meadows and calm waters. He will guide us on the best path for the journey He has planned for our lives.

53

THE GOOD SHEPHERD

The Lord is my shepherd, I lack nothing. . . .
Even though I walk through the darkest valley, I will fear no evil, for you are with me; your rod and your staff, they comfort me.

Psalm 23:1, 4 NIV

The German shepherd dog breed originated in Germany in the late 1800s. It was specifically bred to herd sheep and protect them from predators. A human shepherd keeps the sheep safe from harmful situations, such as wandering too near a cliff or being attacked by dangerous animals. In biblical times (and even today), shepherds led their sheep to grassy fields and near streams so the sheep could graze. They often stood between their sheep and the danger. If a sheep ends up in a bad place, the shepherd uses the hook on the end of his staff to pull the sheep back. Jesus is our shepherd. When we stay close to Him, He leads us to good places and protects us from harm.

54

HIS GOODNESS AND LOVE

You prepare a table before me in the presence of my enemies. You anoint my head with oil; my cup overflows. Surely your goodness and love will follow me all the days of my life, and I will dwell in the house of the Lord forever.

Psalm 23:5–6 NIV

When someone bullies us or tries to harm us, in the moment it can feel like they won. But God will always have the final say. When we follow Him, He will lift us up and give us an honored place while our enemies watch. That may mean winning an award, or it may mean leading us down a peaceful, successful path in life. The focus here isn't on the enemy, though—it's on our Father. When we keep our eyes on God and stay as close to Him as possible, His goodness and love follow us wherever we go. He loves us more than we can imagine.

55

FIND SAFETY IN GOD

Fearing people is a dangerous trap,
but trusting the LORD means safety.
PROVERBS 29:25 NLT

Our peers are the people we do life with. It can refer to others in our age group or simply people in our community. Sometimes we can feel pressure to fit in, even if that means going against our own values or desires. That's what peer pressure is. If you feel tempted to behave in a way that goes against your beliefs or could damage your relationship with God, that can be tough. But when we trust God completely and ask Him for help, He will always provide a way for us to escape that temptation. Sometimes, this means giving us the courage to say no. Other times, He may send a trusted adult or friend along to offer support. Don't be afraid of what others think. Cling to God and He will take care of you.

56

THE FULL STORY

Martha was working hard getting the supper ready. She came to Jesus and said, "Do You see that my sister is not helping me? Tell her to help me."

LUKE 10:40 NLV

It's easy to compare ourselves to others. Whether we're measuring who's prettier, smarter, or who works harder, comparison is a slippery slope that leads to a sandpit of discontent. In the story above, Martha was angry that her sister Mary wasn't working as hard as she was. But Martha didn't know the whole story. She thought Mary was being lazy, but she wasn't. Mary was spending time with her Savior. Mary had a need that could only be met through Christ. God wants us to concern ourselves with Him—pleasing Him, obeying Him, and serving Him and others. What anyone else has or does isn't our concern. Like Martha, we usually don't have the full story anyway.

57

CHOOSING WHAT IS BEST

Jesus said to her, "Martha, Martha, you are worried and troubled about many things. Only a few things are important, even just one. Mary has chosen the good thing. It will not be taken away from her."
LUKE 10:41–42 NLV

Can you picture Jesus shaking His head at Martha, gently redirecting her thoughts? He had compassion. He knew she was frustrated. But she needed this reminder that worry and anxiety don't improve anything. They usually only make things worse. Close your eyes for a moment and listen to Him speaking to *you*. Replace Martha's name with *your* name. Are you choosing what's best, like Mary? Are you focusing your attention and energy on God alone? Or are you like Martha, stressing about things that are out of your control? Listen to His gentle, compassionate voice, pulling you away from your fear and stress and toward His peace.

58

ALL KINDS OF TROUBLES

"But the time is coming—indeed it's here now—when you will be scattered, each one going his own way, leaving me alone. Yet I am not alone because the Father is with me. I have told you all this so that you may have peace in me. Here on earth you will have many trials and sorrows. But take heart, because I have overcome the world."

JOHN 16:32–33 NLT

Staying close to God and following Christ doesn't take away our problems. We live in a fallen, broken, sin-filled world, and while we're here, we'll have all kinds of troubles. Sometimes, we create our own problems because we choose sin and disobedience. Other times, we deal with issues we have no control over. Jesus didn't promise an easy life. Instead, He promised a victorious life. When we focus on Him instead of our problems, He will guide us through each situation with strength, confidence, and peace.

59

YOUR SAFE PLACE

He who takes refuge in the shelter of the Most High will be safe in the shadow of the Almighty. He will say to the Eternal, "My shelter, my mighty fortress, my God, I place all my trust in You."

PSALM 91:1–2 VOICE

When faced with problems, humans have some natural responses. We can fight, run away, or freeze and hope the problems take care of themselves. Though those reactions may help sometimes—after all, God created those responses in us—they should always be paired with complete trust in God. Whatever your situation, cry out to God. He hears you, whether you call to Him out loud or in your head. He has promised never to leave you or turn His back on you. His love and compassion turn fierce when one of His beloved children trusts Him. Find your safe place and shelter in the middle of His love.

60

NOTHING TO FEAR

Do not be afraid of the terrors of the night, nor the arrow that flies in the day. Do not dread the disease that stalks in darkness, nor the disaster that strikes at midday.

PSALM 91:5–6 NLT

Picture a bully picking on the weakest kid in the class. The kid is terrified, wondering what the bully will do next. Suddenly, the bully's face turns pale and his eyes get big. He sees something behind his victim...then he turns and runs. The victim turns around and sees his dad—a bodybuilder—with a "don't mess with my child" look on his face. That story belongs to each of us. Satan is a bully, and he sends all kinds of scary things to threaten us. But our all-powerful Father stands over us. Trust Him to protect you from whatever you face. Stand tall. Lift your chin. With God on your side, you have nothing to fear.

61

HE PROTECTS US

He will tell His angels to care for you and keep you in all your ways. They will hold you up in their hands. So your foot will not hit against a stone. You will walk upon the lion and the snake. You will crush under your feet the young lion and the snake.

Psalm 91:11–13 NLV

These verses paint a powerful and dramatic picture of God's care and protection over His children. Some people misunderstand this passage, thinking it means that nothing can ever harm a Christian. While God does protect us, and He sends His angels to watch over us, He also expects us to follow His wisdom. Instead of thinking nothing can hurt us, we can interpret these verses (and others) as a promise that for those who follow Him, God won't let anything stand in the way of us completing our purpose here on earth.

62

I WILL BE WITH THEM

"When they call on me, I will answer;
I will be with them in trouble. I will rescue
and honor them. I will reward them with a
long life and give them my salvation."

PSALM 91:15–16 NLT

Read the words above carefully. These are God's own words. They are His promise to His children when they call on Him and trust His care for them. Notice that He doesn't promise to keep us free from trouble. Instead, He promises to be with us in our troubles. He promises to rescue us from being defeated by Satan. He also promises that those who follow Him will find great purpose and satisfaction in their lives. We can face our troubles on our own, getting through them with fear and anxiety, or we can trust God, having confidence in His love and care for us. Trusting Him is always the better option.

63

PROMISES FOR THE RIGHTEOUS

For the Eternal watches over the righteous, and His ears are attuned to their prayers. He is always listening. . . . When the upright need help and cry to the Eternal, He hears their cries and rescues them from all of their troubles. When someone is hurting or brokenhearted, the Eternal moves in close and revives him in his pain.

PSALM 34:15, 17–18 VOICE

These promises are for the righteous. A righteous person is someone who does what is right in God's eyes. This doesn't mean we have to be perfect—Jesus was the only perfect human. God doesn't expect us to be perfect—He knows us better than that. But He does want us to always think about Him and how to please Him. That means trusting Him even when it doesn't make sense. It means loving others even when it's hard. It means doing the right thing even when no one is looking. And it means admitting when we've messed up and asking for forgiveness.

64

PROMISE OR PRINCIPLE?

Does anyone want to live a life that is long and prosperous? Then keep your tongue from speaking evil and your lips from telling lies! Turn away from evil and do good. Search for peace, and work to maintain it.

PSALM 34:12–14 NLT

The Bible is filled with God's promises. But it's also filled with principles, or guidelines. It's easy to get the two confused. A promise is like a contract. God always keeps His promises. The verses above contain a principle. Honest and godly people still struggle sometimes. They may not always feel prosperous or successful in life. But we're a whole lot more likely to live a peaceful, contented, productive life when we model ourselves after God's standards. When we lie and cheat and get involved in evil, sinful things, we're much more likely to face the harsh results of those decisions. You're much more likely to feel satisfied with your life when you choose honesty, kindness, and love.

65

PRAISE GOD INSTEAD

I will praise the Lord at all times. I will constantly speak his praises. I will boast only in the Lord; let all who are helpless take heart. Come, let us tell of the Lord's greatness; let us exalt his name together.

PSALM 34:1–3 NLT

David wrote these verses. If anyone had reason for stress and anxiety, it was David. Through no fault of his own, he was on the run from King Saul for years. He feared for his life, even though he'd done nothing wrong. Saul was jealous of David, and he wanted to kill the younger man. Even though David lived through some serious troubles, he praised God. Time and again, God protected him from harm. David knew that praise brought him closer into God's presence. When you face troubles, don't give in to anxiety. Praise God instead. Talk about His goodness and love and experience the peace God gives to those who trust Him with all their hearts.

66

YOUR FOREVER HOME

"God will take away all their tears.
There will be no more death or sorrow or crying
or pain. All the old things have passed away."
REVELATION 21:4 NLV

Do you remember when you were in kindergarten, and it seemed like an eternity before you'd be a teenager? Now you probably look back at that time and wonder where the years went. As you look forward now, it may seem like eons before you are an "old" person. But someday you will look backward and realize just how fast your life has flown by. As a believer in Christ, you will one day live with Him in heaven. At that time, He will wipe away every tear and stress and sorrow from your time on earth, and you will exist in the middle of His love and peace for eternity. When life seems hard, remind yourself this is temporary. Smile at the thought of your forever home that He's prepared with you in mind.

67

WHERE PEACE COMES FROM

Now may the Lord of peace Himself grant you His peace (the peace of His kingdom) at all times and in all ways [under all circumstances and conditions, whatever comes]. The Lord [be] with you all.

2 THESSALONIANS 3:16 AMPC

Paul spent a lot of time writing letters. Much of the New Testament comes from his letters to different people and churches. In this verse, Paul reminded his readers that when we stay close to God, He gives us peace—even when life is hard. His presence in our lives is stable and strong, and the more we lean on Him, the more settled and confident we feel. God will never leave us, but sometimes we walk away from Him. Then we wonder where all the stress and anxiety and fear and depression come from. Those are issues every Christian will face to some degree but staying close to God helps keep it under control.

68

CLEANING OUR HEARTS

Investigate my life, O God, find out everything about me; cross-examine and test me, get a clear picture of what I'm about; see for yourself whether I've done anything wrong—then guide me on the road to eternal life.

PSALM 139:23–24 MSG

Have you ever cleaned your room perfectly, top to bottom, inside the closet and under the bed, and felt so proud of how it looked? It may have stayed that way for a while—anywhere from an hour to a few days or weeks. But eventually, you looked around and realized the clutter and mess had crept back in. That always seems to happen when we don't pay attention. The same is true with sin. As Christians, we can never stop paying attention. In these verses, David asks God to help him identify any sin-clutter in his life. Like David, we should ask God to help us examine our spirits, revealing anything that doesn't need to be there.

69

HANGING OUT WITH GOD

Where can I go from Your Spirit? Or where can I run away from where You are? If I go up to heaven, You are there! If I make my bed in the place of the dead, You are there! If I take the wings of the morning or live in the farthest part of the sea, even there Your hand will lead me and Your right hand will hold me.

PSALM 139:7–10 NLV

Have you ever felt alone in a crowded room? That can be one of the loneliest feelings. But if you have just one friend, it makes all the difference in your comfort level. In our minds, we know God is always with us, but that information doesn't always translate into our emotions, especially when we're anxious. The truth is that God, the King of kings, loves to hang out with you. Wherever you go, He's right there encouraging you, listening to your troubles, and reminding you that He thinks you're fantastic.

70

GOD ADORES YOU

How precious to me are your thoughts, God! How vast is the sum of them! Were I to count them, they would outnumber the grains of sand—when I awake, I am still with you.

Psalm 139:17–18 NIV

God thinks about you all the time. Like, *all the time.* You might even say He is obsessed with you—in a good way. Every moment of every day, He thinks of ways to make you feel loved. While you sleep, He thinks about what a great idea you were and how glad He is He made you. When you wake up, He's still thinking about you. There is no possible way we can humanly measure God's love for us—it's that big, and it keeps growing. Next time you feel insignificant or overlooked, remind yourself of these verses. God adores you. He has loved you for every moment of your existence, and He will love you forever.

71

THINK ABOUT THIS

"Be still, and know that I am God! I will be honored by every nation. I will be honored throughout the world."
PSALM 46:10 NLT

Some of the words used to describe that anxious feeling are jittery, unsettled, and agitated. None of those words paint a picture of stillness. In contrast, visions of a still lake give the impression of peace and serenity. When God tells us to be still and know that He is God, He's asking us to calm our spirits. In stillness, as we think about who He is and what He can do, our anxiety is replaced with peace. Imagine the time when every person in every nation on earth will honor God with their whole hearts. That time is coming. As His daughter, you play an important role in His kingdom. Think about who He is and who you are in Him and let His calm confidence soak into every fiber and every cell of your being.

72

TRUSTING AND WAITING

But those who trust in the Eternal One will regain their strength. They will soar on wings as eagles. They will run—never winded, never weary. They will walk—never tired, never faint.

ISAIAH 40:31 VOICE

Some translations of this verse say "wait" instead of "trust." Trusting someone has an element of waiting to it. It means something hasn't happened yet, but we know it will happen because we believe in the person. It's the confidence we feel, knowing our best friend will save us a seat at the lunch table or that our parents will pick us up from school. While even a friend or a parent may let us down sometimes, God never will. When we wait on Him, believing He will do what He's promised, that trust breeds strength and confidence. It helps us keep going, even when life is hard—with our chins up, our shoulders back, and a smile on our faces.

73

LAUGH TO FEEL BETTER

A glad heart is good medicine,
but a broken spirit dries up the bones.
PROVERBS 17:22 NLV

You may have heard that laughter is good medicine. That's not just a cute phrase. It's actually backed by science. Laughing causes us to relax and relieves tension. It lowers our stress hormones, releases feel-good hormones called endorphins, and increases blood flow. Researchers have found that on average, people who laugh more tend to live longer. Laughter isn't just good for physical health—it elevates mental health and improves social relationships too. And here's the crazy thing—even fake laughter offers those benefits. Next time you feel anxious and sad, try to laugh. Watch a funny video. Think of a happy memory when you giggled a lot. Ask your brother, sister, or friend to tell you a joke. Even if you have to pretend to laugh at first, something will switch in your brain and help you feel better. God loves you and He made you for joy.

74

OPPORTUNITY FOR JOY

Dear brothers and sisters, when troubles of any kind come your way, consider it an opportunity for great joy. For you know that when your faith is tested, your endurance has a chance to grow. So let it grow, for when your endurance is fully developed, you will be perfect and complete, needing nothing.

JAMES 1:2–4 NLT

Hold on. Is James really telling us we should be happy about our problems? No thanks! But that's not actually what he's saying. He says when we face problems, we should be joyful. Joy and happiness aren't the same. Happiness is an emotion based on our current circumstances. Joy is a state of pleasant contentment we experience because we know everything will work out for our best. Part of that involves building our faith, our strength, and our endurance to trust God no matter what comes. When we face trials, we can view them as preparation for the great things God has in store for our lives.

75

MADE FOR VICTORY

Happy is the person who can hold up under the trials of life. At the right time, he'll know God's sweet approval and will be crowned with life. As God has promised, the crown awaits all who love Him.

JAMES 1:12 VOICE

God made us for victory. Satan hates that. Satan wants us to live miserable, defeated lives. He throws all kinds of problems at us, from our grades to our hormones to divorce to deep, gut-wrenching loss. As long as we live in this world, we will face problems. But those problems don't have to win. God is always right there with us, fighting for us and giving us the tools to fight for ourselves. Romans 8:37 says that He made us more than conquerors. When life knocks you down, get back up. Keep going. You already know the end of the story—you're on the winning team. God already has your crown waiting.

76

WHAT TO WEAR

Here is the bottom line: do not worry about your life. Don't worry about what you will eat or what you will drink. Don't worry about how you clothe your body. Living is about more than merely eating, and the body is about more than dressing up.

MATTHEW 6:25 VOICE

We're all prone to worry about what others think. But for many, the most intense period of this concern happens when we're teens. We're still growing, figuring out who we are, and we tend to look around and compare ourselves to others to see how we measure up. We want to carry the mug from the popular coffee shop and wear clothes that tell others we fit in. That's okay, to a degree. It's part of our journey. But never forget that your value comes from your lineage—and your Father is the King! Don't concern yourself too much with what you'll eat or wear. Trust your Father to provide and find your worth in Him alone.

77

HE WILL PROVIDE

Look at the birds in the sky. They do not store food for winter. They don't plant gardens. They do not sow or reap—and yet, they are always fed because your heavenly Father feeds them. And you are even more precious to Him than a beautiful bird. If He looks after them, of course He will look after you.

MATTHEW 6:26 VOICE

A wise person takes advantage of opportunities today to prepare for tomorrow. This verse isn't telling us not to plan for our future. Rather, Jesus reminds us here that we shouldn't *worry* about the future. If you're able, get an education. Learn some skills. Do what you need to do to ensure you can provide for your family and serve others. But don't stress about what will happen next week, next month, or years from now. Serve Him today. Love others today. Trust that He will open the doors He wants opened for you when the time is right. He will provide.

78

QUALITY OF LIFE

"Can all your worries add a single moment to your life?"
MATTHEW 6:27 NLT

Worry puts us into a state of panic. It often leaves us frozen in fear, or it sends us into a nervous hive of activity. Our stomachs get all knotted up, and we snap at other people. None of those things contribute to the length or quality of our lives. Instead of worrying, pray. Tell God what's on your mind. Then trust Him and obey that gentle voice—His Holy Spirit. Calm, wise action takes discipline. But as with all things, it gets easier with practice. When you find yourself being pulled back into worry, take a deep breath, center your thoughts on God, and do what He says. Repeat that as many times as you need to. Then watch the quality of your life increase as He fills you with His peace, joy, and confidence.

79

DRESSING LIKE A QUEEN

"Why worry about your clothing? Look at the lilies of the field and how they grow. They don't work or make their clothing, yet Solomon in all his glory was not dressed as beautifully as they are. And if God cares so wonderfully for wildflowers that are here today and thrown into the fire tomorrow, he will certainly care for you. Why do you have so little faith?"

MATTHEW 6:28–30 NLT

Here, Jesus focuses on the flowers, comparing their colorful beauty to the clothes we wear. God will provide everything we need to hold our heads high and feel good about ourselves in Him. While the flowers don't have to do anything to look beautiful, God does want us to care for the clothing He provides by keeping it clean and folded or hung. Often, dressing like a queen means getting something new or thrifted, but sometimes it means simply valuing the things we already have.

80

RELAX IN HIM

"What I'm trying to do here is to get you to relax, to not be so preoccupied with getting, so you can respond to God's giving. People who don't know God and the way he works fuss over these things, but you know both God and how he works. Steep your life in God-reality, God-initiative, God-provisions. Don't worry about missing out. You'll find all your everyday human concerns will be met."

MATTHEW 6:31–33 MSG

It goes against our nature to just let go and trust God...but that's exactly what He asks us to do. He doesn't want us to get trapped in a worry loop. Instead, He calls us to step into a new reality—one of freedom, peace, and joy. When we share our concerns with God and leave it to Him to deal with them, we are free to simply relax. Then we can find purpose and joy in serving Him and others with the unique gifts He's given us.

81

IT'S ALL UNDER CONTROL

"Do not let your heart be troubled. You have put your trust in God, put your trust in Me also."

JOHN 14:1 NLV

Just before this verse, in Chapter 13, Jesus tried to explain what was about to happen. He would be betrayed, arrested, and crucified. When Peter promised to defend Jesus to the end, Jesus responded by telling Peter that he would actually deny even knowing Jesus three times before morning! As you can imagine, the disciples were upset by this. That's when Jesus said, "It's okay. Don't worry about it. This thing we're facing? It's temporary. Trust me that it will all work out the way it's supposed to in the end." Jesus told them He was going to prepare a place in heaven for them, and that one day they'd join Him there. He makes that same promise to us. Whatever you face, remember it's temporary. Remember God loves you. And remember He has it all under control.

82

TRUST HIS WORD

"For no word from God will ever fail."
LUKE 1:37 NIV

In order to fully understand this verse, you need some backstory. An angel had just told Mary she was expecting Jesus, the Son of God. Mary was confused, because she'd never been with a man in that way. How could she be pregnant? The angel told her it was possible through the Holy Spirit. It was possible because God would make it happen. God isn't limited by human reason or the laws of reproduction and genetics. He is all-powerful, and anything He says goes! That's why it's so important to study God's Word, the Bible. God will always make good on His promises. But we have to do our part by believing those promises—that belief is called *faith*. What problem do you face? What seems impossible to you? Make it your goal to find out what God has to say about it. Then trust Him to keep His Word, which is always based in love.

83

DON'T BE DISCOURAGED

Joshua said to them, "Do not be afraid; do not be discouraged. Be strong and courageous."
JOSHUA 10:25 NIV

When Moses died, Joshua became the Israelites' next leader. He would lead them into the Promised Land. Joshua was young. He'd never been in charge of leading a nation. It was normal for him to be anxious. But God told Joshua to be strong and courageous. He reminded Joshua not to get discouraged, because no matter what happened, no matter what he faced, God would be with him. God makes the same promise to us. Imagine the king of Kings calling you by name. "Be strong and courageous! Don't be afraid or discouraged. I will be with you wherever you go." When anxiety kicks in, listen for those words and picture the almighty, all-powerful warrior king walking beside you, clearing the path for all the good things He has in store for your life.

84

DON'T WORRY. BE HAPPY.

Which one of you can add a single hour to your life or 18 inches to your height by worrying really hard?

LUKE 12:25 VOICE

You can almost hear a little humor in Jesus' voice as you read those words. Have you ever worried yourself into being taller or shorter? Can you worry hard enough to make your life longer? Of course not. It's a ridiculous thought. Yet so many of us spend *way* too much time worrying about things we have no control over. Instead of worrying, Jesus wants us to live carefree lives, trusting God completely for all our needs. Of course He also wants us to be responsible, work hard, and use the gifts He's given us. But in all those things, He wants us to have joy, not anxiety. Next time you find yourself worrying about something, ask yourself if you're doing what God wants you to do. Are you loving Him? Are you loving others? Concern yourself with those things, and trust God for everything else.

85

THE WATER SOURCE

But blessed is the one who trusts in Me alone; the Eternal will be his confidence. He is like a tree planted by water, sending out its roots beside the stream. It does not fear the heat or even drought. Its leaves stay green and its fruit is dependable, no matter what it faces.

JEREMIAH 17:7–8 VOICE

When drilling a well, machines bore a hole deep into the ground. The source of water, deep in the earth, won't dry up. That's why trees that have deep roots near a water source do fine even in a drought. They don't rely on surface water for nourishment. They are tapped into the source.

God is our source! When we put our trust in Him, we grow strong roots that will never run dry. But when we trust in other things, those sources of confidence and security will eventually shrivel up, and we'll be left parched and dehydrated. Let God be your source of strength and confidence.

THE MINUTE YOU CALL

The minute I said, "I'm slipping, I'm falling,"
your love, God, took hold and held me fast.
When I was upset and beside myself, you
calmed me down and cheered me up.

Psalm 94:18–19 MSG

Experts disagree about who wrote this psalm. Some say David is the author, while many others think it was someone else—but they're not sure who. It's actually good that we don't know, because these words could have been said by any of us. God's response is true for all of us. Are you slipping? Do you feel like you're falling? Tell God! The author says God rescued him "the minute [he] said, 'I'm slipping, I'm falling.'" God created us to have a relationship with Him. He wants us to talk to Him. Picture Him waiting by the phone, longing for us to call. The moment He hears your voice, He is already there, loving you, calming you, and giving you peace.

87

CONTRACT OF PEACE

You will guard him and keep him in perfect and constant peace whose mind [both its inclination and its character] is stayed on You, because he commits himself to You, leans on You, and hopes confidently in You.

ISAIAH 26:3 AMPC

When someone hires a person to do a job, there's often a contract involved. The employer pays the worker to complete a task. If the worker doesn't do what they're hired to do, the employer isn't obligated to pay. God's promise of peace is like a contract. When we fulfill our end of the agreement by keeping our minds focused on Him and living to please Him, He gives us peace. But when we do whatever we want without thinking about God, His peace is hard to find. We end up living in anxiety and depression, anger and fear. Are you missing peace in your life? Try shifting your focus to your Father, multiple times a day, as many times as it takes.

NEVER LETTING GO

"That's right. Because I, your God, have a firm grip on you and I'm not letting go. I'm telling you, 'Don't panic. I'm right here to help you.'"

Isaiah 41:13 MSG

What a comforting thought this is! God has us. He's holding on tight. We are precious to Him, and He's not about to let us go. You may have heard that God won't give you more than you can handle, but that's not necessarily true. It's better to remember you won't ever go through anything that *He* can't handle. Whatever we face, God's right there. Even if the problem seems too big for us, we don't need to panic. Whether we face a difficult test or a frightening health diagnosis, a fight with our friend or the loss of a loved one, God has us securely in His arms. We can relax, cozy into His love, and know that He has us in His grip. He's got everything under control.

89

NOW AND THEN

"Count on it: Everyone who had it in for you will end up out in the cold—real losers. Those who worked against you will end up empty-handed—nothing to show for their lives. When you go out looking for your old adversaries you won't find them—not a trace of your old enemies, not even a memory."

ISAIAH 41:11–12 MSG

These words were written to Israel. The nation of Israel had many enemies who wanted to destroy it. But while the people of Israel saw only what was happening right then, God already knew the future. He knew that in the end, everything would work out for the best. The same is true for us as individuals. Sometimes it feels like our enemies will win, but that's because we can only see what's happening right now. God promises that in the end, His children will win—both in this life and in eternity.

90

DON'T GIVE UP

So let's not allow ourselves to get fatigued doing good. At the right time we will harvest a good crop if we don't give up, or quit. Right now, therefore, every time we get the chance, let us work for the benefit of all, starting with the people closest to us in the community of faith.

GALATIANS 6:9–10 MSG

Do you ever get tired of doing the right thing? It can seem like people who make *wrong* choices have more fun. But selfish, sinful choices bring regrets. When we choose to serve ourselves instead of serving God and others, our lives become shallow and disappointing. It goes against our human nature to choose a life of service, but we must do it anyway. Love God, even when it's hard. Love others, even when they're annoying. Keep doing the good things God puts in your path. When you make those little choices, they add up and lead to a lifetime of purpose, contentment, and joy.

91

ALL THAT MATTERS

Oh Martha, Martha, you are so anxious and concerned about a million details, but really, only one thing matters. Mary has chosen that one thing, and I won't take it away from her.

LUKE 10:41–42 VOICE

Martha often gets a bad reputation. After all, she was trying to serve others. She was cleaning up, preparing the food, and doing all the good things that needed to be done. Many of us do the same—we get so distracted doing *good* things, we forget to do the *best* thing. If we're not careful, we can get caught up in the anxiety of doing *all the things.* Our intentions are good, but anytime we make *things* more important that worshipping God, we're not getting it right. Martha was so concerned about her to-do list she became grumpy with her sister. She even tattled to Jesus! When you find yourself stressed out over the little things, go back to the most important thing: loving God with all your heart.

92

I WILL TRUST

When I am afraid, I will trust in You.

PSALM 56:3 NLV

David wrote these words. Much of his life was spent on the run from those who wanted to kill him—first, King Saul and later, his own son. This simple, straightforward sentence is easy to memorize. Read it out loud several times. Now look away and say it without looking. Write it on a small card you can pull out if you forget and keep it in your pocket or your purse. When anxiety ties your stomach into knots, when you feel tight and have trouble breathing, say these words, just as King David did. "When I am afraid, I will trust in You." To trust someone means to believe they are reliable, strong, and true. Do you believe God is reliable and strong? Do you believe He's true to His Word? Focus on that belief, knowing He will always take care of you, because He loves you so much.

93

THE WINNING TEAM

"In this godless world you will continue to experience difficulties. But take heart! I've conquered the world."

JOHN 16:33 MSG

Some people think that if we follow Christ and love God with all our hearts, we won't have any problems. But that's not true at all! Jesus was without sin. He loved God more than anything, yet He ended up on the cross. Take a look at the disciples and the Old Testament prophets and you'll find people who faced many hardships. Troubles and difficulties are part of the package as we go through life. The difference for Christ-followers is that the problems won't win—unless we let them. When we choose to stay close to Christ, He gives us strength for the fight and endurance for the journey. He gives us joy and hope for good things to come. When you face trials, remember that you are a warrior, fighting for the winning team, and your king has already declared victory.

94

IN THE DARK VALLEY

Even when I walk through the darkest valley,
I will not be afraid, for you are close beside me.
Your rod and your staff protect and comfort me.
PSALM 23:4 NLT

Psalm 23 is one of the most memorized and most quoted scriptures in the Bible. That's probably because so many people can relate to David's emotions in this chapter. David walked through some pretty dark times—and so will we. But David knew he didn't have to be afraid, because God was right there with him, fighting for him, protecting him, and holding him close to comfort his anxiety. When you find yourself in David's shoes, walking a dark, difficult path, bring this picture to mind. God is right there with you. He's fighting for you, protecting you, and wrapping His strong, loving arms around you to calm your anxiety. You don't have to be afraid.

95

FORCING AWAY THE FEAR

May the God of your hope so fill you with all joy and peace in believing [through the experience of your faith] that by the power of the Holy Spirit you may abound and be overflowing (bubbling over) with hope.

ROMANS 15:13 AMPC

Anxiety is an overwhelming emotion. When it takes over, it fills every part of us, leaving no room for anything else. It can cripple us, leaving us paralyzed so we can't function at our best. But there's good news for those who struggle with this kind of fear. God's presence is stronger and thicker and denser. When we let Him in, He takes over, crowding out the anxiety and replacing it with His joy, peace, and confidence. That doesn't mean God is pushy. He doesn't force Himself on us. We must choose Him. We must invite Him in. When we do, He shows up with His massive, all-consuming love, and in His presence, all the darkness, fear, and anxiety flee.

96

THAT IS FAITH

Now faith is confidence in what we hope for and assurance about what we do not see. This is what the ancients were commended for.

HEBREWS 11:1–2 NIV

Think about your favorite chair. Do you ever look at that chair and think, *I wonder if that thing will hold me up?* Probably not. You just sit down with full confidence it's not going to break and send you crashing to the ground. Each time you sit in the chair, you show faith. God wants us to have that kind of confidence in Him. He wants us to come to Him with our problems without wondering if He'll take care of us. We simply "sit" in His love, knowing He will hold us up. People in the Old Testament, like Abraham, were confident God would send the Messiah long before Jesus ever came. That was faith. How confident are you that God loves you and will take care of you, no matter what comes?

97

WHOM SHOULD I FEAR?

So what should we say about all of this? If God is on our side, then tell me: whom should we fear?

ROMANS 8:31 VOICE

Think of fictional superheroes in the movies or on television—heroes like Wonder Woman or Iron Man or Captain America. If a bad guy shows up, you might be afraid. You might worry that the bad guy is too strong for you. But if one of those heroes swooped in, you'd breathe a sigh of relief, knowing they're bigger and stronger and will protect you. One cool thing about being a Christian is that our hero isn't fictional. God chooses to make His home inside our hearts. That means He is always with us. He is bigger than any problem and stronger than any bully. There's no circumstance too hard for Him. If God is on our side, whom should we fear?

Nothing and no one. That's who.

98

WATCH YOUR LANGUAGE!

Don't use foul or abusive language. Let everything you say be good and helpful, so that your words will be an encouragement to those who hear them.

EPHESIANS 4:29 NLT

Cursing and foul language have become so common in our culture, many people don't even notice it anymore. Words and phrases that were once considered offensive are now routine and ordinary, even among Christians. Does that mean it's okay? The Bible says it's not. Our words give a peek into our hearts and let others know clues about our character. When we say we're Christians but we use rude, vulgar language, we send a mixed message. Coarse language doesn't promote the peaceful life God wants for His children. Instead of cursing, try finding ways to encourage others with your words. Your calm way of communication will settle your spirit, inspire those around you, and communicate God's qualities of love and kindness.

HIS CREATIVE PROCESS

We know that God makes all things work together for the good of those who love Him and are chosen to be a part of His plan.

ROMANS 8:28 NLV

This is an encouraging verse, for sure. It's also often misunderstood. These words don't mean that everything is good. They don't even mean that everything we face is part of God's perfect plan for our lives. Sometimes we make poor choices, and we have to endure the consequences. And sometimes others do things that affect us in a negative way. But through it all, God is still God. He is the Creator, which means that no matter how bitter the ingredients, He can turn it into something sweet. He will use whatever junk life throws at us and make something beautiful and useful for His purpose. Trust Him. Trust the process. Then wait with expectation as the Creator does His work in your life.

100

AN ACCURATE PICTURE

When I walk into the thick of trouble,
keep me alive in the angry turmoil. With one
hand strike my foes, with your other hand
save me. Finish what you started in me, God.
Your love is eternal—don't quit on me now.
Psalm 138:7–8 MSG

David has such a beautiful way of using words to capture an image of God. When you have trouble picturing how God may be working, turn to the Psalms for inspiration. Here, we see God holding David safely with one hand while He wallops the enemy with His other fist. What a great vision, especially when we're overcome with anxiety. Many scriptures tell us God holds us in His hand (see Isaiah 41:10, for one). He also promises many times to defeat our enemies—those who stand in the way of our living out His good purpose for our lives (see Psalm 18:37–50). David's imagery is accurate, based on God's promises. Claim those promises for yourself.

101

WHEN I'M WEAK

But he said to me, "My grace is sufficient for you, for my power is made perfect in weakness." Therefore I will boast all the more gladly about my weaknesses, so that Christ's power may rest on me. That is why, for Christ's sake, I delight in weaknesses, in insults, in hardships, in persecutions, in difficulties. For when I am weak, then I am strong.

2 Corinthians 12:9–10 NIV

On its own, verse 10 sounds kind of strange. Why would anyone delight in insults, hardship, persecution, or difficulty? But paired with verse 9, it makes perfect sense. When we're strong on our own, we may rely on ourselves too much. God gets pushed to the side, and since He doesn't force us to follow Him, He lets us do our thing. Without God, this isn't usually much to brag about. But when we're weak, we tend to lean more on God. That's when He cracks His knuckles, flexes His muscles, and lets His power soar.

102

WHY GOD GOES BEFORE US

"The Lord himself goes before you and will be with you; he will never leave you nor forsake you. Do not be afraid; do not be discouraged."
DEUTERONOMY 31:8 NIV

If you've ever watched a police detective show, you've probably seen one officer go ahead of the others, waving the others forward or signaling them to stay back. The officer in front scopes out the safety of the situation for the others to protect them from unnecessary harm. That's what God does for us. When we look to Him and follow His lead, we are protected from unnecessary harm. But when we ignore His direction and move ahead of Him, we often face unneeded hardship and regrets. Trust His guidance. He knows better than you do what lies ahead, and He will never leave you to make those decisions alone. When we rely on God instead of ourselves, we never have reason to be afraid.

103

WANT VS. NEED

God is able to bless you abundantly, so that in all things at all times, having all that you need, you will abound in every good work.

2 CORINTHIANS 9:8 NIV

Have you ever felt like you needed chocolate? Most of us have been there. But deep down, we know chocolate is more of a want than a need. We need air, water, and nourishment. We need clothing and shelter. Depending on where we live, we may need transportation. And we often need supplies to do our work as a student or at our after-school job. God has a purpose for each of us, and when we align ourselves with that purpose, He will give us everything we need—abundantly—to do all the good things He wants us to do. Ask God to change your desires to match His and watch how He provides all you need.

104

THIS IS LOVE

"For this is how God loved the world: He gave his one and only Son, so that everyone who believes in him will not perish but have eternal life. God sent his Son into the world not to judge the world, but to save the world through him."

JOHN 3:16–17 NLT

Think of the person you love most in this world. Would you sacrifice that person's life to save a bunch of strangers who don't care about you? Of course you wouldn't. Yet that's exactly what God did. God is full of compassion, and He knew that without some intervention, we had no hope. The punishment for sin is death, or separation from God, because God can't be in the presence of sin. He knew we couldn't pay that penalty for ourselves. If we died, we'd stay dead. But Jesus had the power to overcome death. God sent Jesus to pay for our sins so we wouldn't have to. Now *that's* love.

105

ON HIS WAY

With this news, strengthen those who have tired hands, and encourage those who have weak knees. Say to those with fearful hearts, "Be strong, and do not fear, for your God is coming to destroy your enemies. He is coming to save you."

ISAIAH 35:3–4 NLT

If you've ever worked so hard your hands hurt, your back ached, and your legs felt like they wouldn't hold you up anymore, you've had a small taste of what the Israelites may have felt in this passage. They'd been exiled from their homeland and had to work hard as slaves and servants. They were exhausted, and many of them probably felt hopeless. But God told them to lift up their heads. God, who loves His children, was already in the process of rescuing them. When we're tired, whether physically or emotionally, we can lift our heads. God loves you. He sees you. He's already working things out to rescue you.

106

THE HOLY SPIRIT

"When you are put into their hands, do not be afraid of what you are to say or how you are to say it. Whatever is given to you to say at that time, say it. It will not be you who speaks, but the Holy Spirit."

MARK 13:11 NLV

Jesus warned His disciples that they'd face all kinds of troubles for following Him. He knew He'd soon die, be resurrected, and eventually leave them behind to return to heaven. But He wanted them to know He wouldn't leave them alone and defenseless. Though He wouldn't be with them physically, the Holy Spirit would stay with them. We have the Holy Spirit too. When we seek God and try to please Him, the Holy Spirit often speaks to us in a quiet, confident voice in our heads. The more we trust God, the easier it is to hear His Spirit. No matter what you face, don't be afraid. Let the Holy Spirit guide you.

107

WHO GETS THE CREDIT?

When you are tempted to do wrong, do not say, "God is tempting me." God cannot be tempted. He will never tempt anyone.

JAMES 1:13 NLV

It's common for those who don't understand God's character to blame Him for the bad things that happen. But God is good. He is love. He is full of compassion and mercy. When God designed this world, it was for our absolute pleasure as we grew in our relationship with Him. But when sin entered the world, everything went downhill. Bad things happen because we live in a broken world. When we sin, the consequences hurt us. When others sin, their choices impact those around them. One day, God will do away with Satan once and for all. Until then, be sure to give credit where it's due. Bad things like crime, abuse, and disease are a result of Satan's work in this world. James 1:17 tells us every good and perfect gift is from God.

108

SLOW TO GET ANGRY

Understand this, my dear brothers and sisters: You must all be quick to listen, slow to speak, and slow to get angry. Human anger does not produce the righteousness God desires.

JAMES 1:19–20 NLT

Many relationship problems begin with poor communication. We don't really listen when someone else is talking, because we're too busy thinking about the next thing *we* want to say. The other person is probably doing the same thing. We end up talking over each other, louder and louder until our faces are red and our hearts are pounding and we're ready to punch something. This passage in James tells us how we can avoid that scene. When someone else talks, try to clear your mind of what you want to say and really listen. Respond to what they say with love and compassion, and they'll be more likely to do the same.

109

THEN AND NOW

God did not keep His own Son for Himself but gave Him for us all. Then with His Son, will He not give us all things?
ROMANS 8:32 NLV

Paul wrote the book of Romans as a letter to the Christians living in Rome. Some of them came from a Jewish background, and others were Gentiles, or non-Jewish. Regardless of their background, Paul wanted to offer guidance and encouragement for these new believers. He reminded them that if God gave His only Son, Jesus, to pay the price they could never pay for themselves, surely His love was beyond measure. There was nothing God wouldn't do to make sure they were cared for, and that every need was met. God is the same today as He was then. He gave Jesus for you. He will certainly take care of every need you have. He loves you so very much.

110

FOCUS ON GOD

The mind governed by the flesh is death, but the mind governed by the Spirit is life and peace.

Romans 8:6 NIV

Because we're human, our instinct is to look out for the "flesh," or our immediate needs. This often leads us to make selfish choices. It also causes us to be frustrated and angry when we don't get our way. Paul urges us to set aside that natural, human way of thinking and instead focus on the Holy Spirit. God's way of thinking leads us in an entirely different direction than our human nature. When we seek God and make our choices based on what will please Him, we'll live a more relaxed, contented, peaceful life. That doesn't mean we won't have troubles—we will. But focusing on God instead of ourselves gives us an inner confidence and serenity that we can never find without Him.

III

GOODY TWO-SHOES

But even if you suffer for doing what is right, God will reward you for it. So don't worry or be afraid of their threats.

1 PETER 3:14 NLT

The phrase "goody two-shoes" comes from a children's story from the 1700s, in which an orphan girl triumphs over difficulties by doing the right thing. In the story, she was a heroine, but the phrase now has a negative meaning. It implies someone who does the right thing and spoils others' fun. Doing the right thing can be hard, especially when you're going against popular opinion. Not only do you have to resist peer pressure, but you have the aftereffects of having others treat you like you're a nerd or a *goody two-shoes.* But just as the character in the story ended up the victor, doing what's right will bring God's blessings and protection. Always do what pleases God, even if it doesn't please others. You won't regret it.

112

SHIFT IN PERSPECTIVE

The blameless spend their days under the Lord's care, and their inheritance will endure forever. In times of disaster they will not wither; in days of famine they will enjoy plenty. But the wicked will perish: Though the Lord's enemies are like the flowers of the field, they will be consumed, they will go up in smoke.

Psalm 37:18–20 NIV

David wrote this psalm when it felt like the wicked were winning. It seemed to him that even though he always tried to please God, he was constantly on the losing side, while those who chose to live evil, sinful lives had it made. But like the flowers of the field, beautiful today but gone tomorrow, their success is short-lived. Those who live for God will stand strong for all eternity. When it seems like the bad guys are in the lead, shift your perspective. In God's great plan, His children are already the winners.

113

THE FARMER AND THE SEEDS

"The seed falling among the thorns refers to someone who hears the word, but the worries of this life and the deceitfulness of wealth choke the word, making it unfruitful."

MATTHEW 13:22 NIV

Jesus often taught in parables, or stories with a hidden meaning. This parable tells the story of a farmer who casts out seeds into the field. Some land on the road, some on the rocks, some in the weeds and thorns, and some on fertile soil. His disciples asked Him to explain the parable, and Jesus shared what each type of seed represented. We are the seeds...and we get to choose the type of soil we have. When we worry and stress over things instead of trusting God, the worries become our focus. Those things choke out our growing relationship with God. The good news is we can choose to trust God for all our concerns. Ask God to make your heart into fertile soil.

114

SET YOUR MIND

I have set the Lord continually before me; because He is at my right hand, I shall not be moved.

PSALM 16:8 AMPC

Have you ever set your mind on something? To "set your mind" means to focus so completely on something that you don't let anything distract you. If we set our minds to make good grades, our grades will probably improve. If we set our minds to be more organized or to exercise more or wake up earlier, we will make strides. But when we get distracted from our goals, the improvement slows down or stops. When we set the Lord before us, that means we're so focused on Him that we won't let other things distract us from His power, His love, or His plan for our lives. When we do this, He holds our hands, gives us confidence, and helps us succeed in living out His purpose.

115

ON THINGS ABOVE

Set your minds and keep them set on
what is above (the higher things),
not on the things that are on the earth.
COLOSSIANS 3:2 AMPC

Paul encouraged his readers to focus on higher things, not the things of this world. We all have to pay attention to worldly things, like getting dressed, feeding ourselves, and following through with our responsibilities and commitments. But we don't have to make those things the focus of our lives. Our focus, or what we set our minds on, is more about our purpose. We can focus on the negative—noticing bad things, sharing gossip, or filling our minds with stressful thoughts. Or we can push those concerns aside and focus on God and becoming more like Him. God is love. How can we be more loving? God is kind, compassionate, and merciful. How can we show those traits to others? God is strong. How can we exhibit His strength in our lives?

116

THE GOD OF HOPE

"God will take away all their tears.
There will be no more death or sorrow or crying
or pain. All the old things have passed away."
REVELATION 21:4 NLV

Many times in the Bible, God tells us to hope in Him. Hope is the belief that good things are in store. It's not the same as a wish, which is a desire for something good. A *wish* says, "I want this." *Hope* says, "I know this is already in the works." It's appropriate that in Revelation, the final book of the Bible, we're reminded of what's already in the works. As God's children, we have a very real future in which there will be no more tears, sorrow, crying, pain, death, or anxiety of any kind. In the meantime, He will never leave us alone. We have the God of hope to walk through this life and all its seasons with us.

117

TRYING TO IMPRESS

"Be sure you do not do good things in front of others just to be seen by them. If you do, you have no reward from your Father in heaven."
MATTHEW 6:1 NLV

When we concern ourselves more with what others think than what God thinks, it increases our anxiety, because we can't control what anyone else thinks. It may seem easier to do the right thing when we know others will applaud us for it. But if we only do good things when others are watching, so they'll be impressed, we don't impress God at all. He makes it clear that such motives lead to the only reward we'll receive—attention from others. But when we choose what is right even when no one is looking, God will bless us. In verses three and four of this chapter, we're told to do good things in secret. Verse four (NIV) tells us, "Then your Father, who sees what is done in secret, will reward you."

KEEP LIVING FOR GOD

Don't worry about the wicked or envy those who do wrong.

PSALM 37:1 NLT

We humans come up with all kinds of reasons to impress those who aren't living for God. Sometimes we want to please them because they're bullies, and we want them to leave us alone. Other times, we think they're having more fun than we are, and we want to be included in their circle. But God doesn't want us to concern ourselves at all with those who aren't living for God, other than to show them how great He is. Pray for them, but don't worry about them. If it seems like ungodly people are winning at life, remember that things aren't always as they appear. God promises love, kindness, joy, and peace to those who live for Him. Separation from God means the absence of those things in any way that's permanent. Keep living for God—you've chosen the better way.

119

WHERE'S YOUR TREASURE?

Some people store up treasures in their homes here on earth. This is a shortsighted practice—don't undertake it. Moths and rust will eat up any treasure you may store here. Thieves may break into your homes and steal your precious trinkets.

MATTHEW 6:19 VOICE

There's a reality show called *Hoarders*. Each episode highlights someone who has a tough time getting rid of stuff. Many of these people have physical or mental struggles. The people who try to help them on the show are kind and compassionate.

We all have trouble letting go of things sometimes. Our closets are crammed with clothes we don't wear, and our kitchen pantries are filled with expired soup and macaroni. Some people spend far too much time and money trying to get more *stuff*, because they think the stuff will make them happy. But it never does. Don't be one of those people. Get rid of the stuff you don't use, need, or love, and find your joy in loving God and others.

120

HE WILL RESCUE YOU

For He will rescue you from the snares set by your enemies who entrap you and from deadly plagues.

PSALM 91:3 VOICE

Some translations of the Bible say, "He will rescue you from the fowler's snare." A fowler is a person who hunts birds. In biblical times, they set traps to catch birds for their dinner. Have you ever felt like someone was trying to trap you, or set you up to fail? Some people do that because they're insecure and jealous. Others trap people because they have bad motives. When we stay close to God, He promises to rescue us from those people. That may mean staying away from the places the "fowlers" will be or staying near those you know are safe. It may also mean telling a trusted person about what is happening. Ask God for wisdom and guidance to stay safe from those who mean you harm. Listen to His voice and follow His leading.

121

COVERED BY HIS WINGS

Like a bird protecting its young, God will cover you with His feathers, will protect you under His great wings; His faithfulness will form a shield around you, a rock-solid wall to protect you.

PSALM 91:4 VOICE

If you've never seen a bird sheltering its chicks, you should do an internet search for that image. It's a beautiful, touching sight. In the presence of danger, whether it's bad weather or a predator, the mother bird will spread her wings to cover her babies. She will often scoop them beneath her so you can't even see them. She uses her whole body to protect them while they hide safely in her feathers. In the same way, God spreads His presence around us, covering us with His body (through Christ), His strength, and His fierce love. When you feel afraid, remember that picture. He surrounds you, and He will stop at nothing to protect you.

122

IN THE END

A thousand may fall on your left, ten thousand may die on your right, but these horrors won't come near you. Only your eyes will witness the punishment that awaits the evil, but you will not suffer because of it.

PSALM 91:7–8 VOICE

God is serious about protecting those who love Him with all their hearts. That doesn't mean we'll never suffer—we live in a fallen, broken, sin-filled world, and sometimes we'll go through pain and hardship. While it's unpleasant, pain can be a good thing. It can build strength and give wisdom for the future. Difficult times aren't fun while we're in the middle of them, but they help us grow and develop a Christlike character. Though He doesn't cause bad things, God lets us experience discomfort that helps us grow. *But He won't let those things destroy us.* In the end, we'll be the victors over the hard things of this life.

123

A GREATER PURPOSE

If you make the LORD your refuge, if you make the Most High your shelter, no evil will conquer you; no plague will come near your home.

PSALM 91:9–10 NLT

This verse can be misleading when taken out of context. God didn't promise an easy, trouble-free life. Job was a righteous man who experienced great suffering—but only because God had a reason for that suffering. When God says He will protect us, we can be certain that no bad thing will happen to us without God allowing it for a greater purpose. When we trust God and follow Him closely, we can relax, knowing He will keep us safe and secure, ready to fulfill His perfect plan for our lives. And when hard things come, we can rest easy, knowing God has a greater plan even in our difficulties. Any suffering we experience here on earth is temporary. It will one day be replaced with eternal joy.

124

FEAR OR FAITH?

Instantly Jesus reached out His hand and caught and held him, saying to him, O you of little faith, why did you doubt?

MATTHEW 14:31 AMPC

In this passage, Peter has responded to Jesus' invitation to step out of the boat and walk on water. He did it! He let himself fully trust Jesus' power and did something that wasn't humanly possible. Instead of praising Peter's faith, Jesus questioned his *lack* of faith once he started to sink. Why, once he'd already experienced the freedom of fully trusting Christ, did he lose faith again? The answer is fear. Peter allowed fear to control him instead of being controlled by faith. We do the same thing. We start to see God's amazing power in our lives, and it's like we're walking on water. But then we let Satan distract us with fear and anxiety, and we start to sink. What are you letting control you—fear or faith?

125

GOD KNOWS, AND HE UNDERSTANDS

All my longings lie open before you,
Lord; my sighing is not hidden from you.
My heart pounds, my strength fails me;
even the light has gone from my eyes.
PSALM 38:9–10 NIV

It's clear from this passage and others that David struggled with depression. Many of us can relate to the sighing and the heart pounding. In the middle of David's sadness, though, he knew God was there. God knew his thoughts, and He understood. Somehow, the knowledge that someone sees us, knows our struggles, and understands makes our load a little easier to bear. We can draw comfort from David's words, because they are true for us as well. God knows what we're thinking. He knows our struggles. He knows all about our depression, our sadness, our fears, and our anxiety, and He's right there with us. He will never leave us to face those struggles alone.

126

BECAUSE HE LOVES ME

"Because he loves me," says the LORD,
"I will rescue him; I will protect him,
for he acknowledges my name."
PSALM 91:14 NIV

If you ever take a hike in the woods and accidentally stumble upon a group of bear cubs, you'd better run. Get away from that place as fast as you can, because if the mama bear catches you, she won't be kind. She is very protective of her babies, and she's suspicious of any creature—human or otherwise—that could pose a threat. She'll strike first and ask questions later. (Actually, she won't even ask questions at all.) That's kind of how God is with those who love Him. He's extremely protective of those who choose to live for Him. It's not because we're good or smart or pretty or talented. His fierce watchfulness is an outpouring of His love for us, simply because we choose to love Him.

127

MY PAST MISTAKES

My guilt overwhelms me—it is a burden too heavy to bear.

PSALM 38:4 NLT

David felt a lot of anxiety and regret over his past mistakes. It's funny that he was called "a man after God's own heart," yet he was also guilty of adultery and murder. How could God compare such a man to Himself? The good news for David and for us is that once we admit our mistakes, agree with God that we messed up, and ask Him to forgive us, He does! Psalm 103:12 (NIV) says, "As far as the east is from the west, so far has he removed our transgressions from us." He wipes the slate clean. When guilt over past mistakes keeps us awake at night, we must first make sure we've admitted our wrong and asked for forgiveness. Then we can tell Satan to be quiet, because he's the one making us feel guilty—not God.

128

WHAT WE LONG FOR

Take delight in the Lord, and he will give you your heart's desires.

Psalm 37:4 NLT

When you lie in bed at night, and everything is quiet, what do you long for? Is it a certain friendship, a fancy wardrobe, or an exciting vacation? Maybe you dream of a certain career or future situation. God knows our desires. Nothing is hidden from Him. As long as those desires aren't sinful, they're not wrong. They become sinful when they directly go against God's definition of right and wrong, or when we place them above our relationship with Him. Talk to God about your wants, your hopes, and your dreams. Ask Him to adjust your goals to match up with His plans for you. Ask Him to change your priorities if needed. Then relax into His love for you, knowing He wants even better things for you than you want for yourself.

129

CALL HIS NAME

Do not leave me alone, O Lord!
O my God, do not be far from me!
Hurry to help me, O Lord, Who saves me!
PSALM 38:21–22 NLV

One of the worst feelings is being all alone when we're upset or anxious. No matter how bad things are, if we even have one person with us supporting us and helping us through, things seem just a little bit better. If another human can have that effect, just think what God will do! The good news is, even when we *feel* alone, we aren't. God promises never to leave us or turn His back on us. When we call out to Him, He rushes to remind us of His presence, His power, and His love. Next time you feel alone, call His name, like David did in these verses. Ask Him to give you strength and courage. Then wait for Him to show up and show off in your life.

130

NO MATTER WHAT

My heart beats fast. My strength leaves me.
Even the light of my eyes has gone from me.
My loved ones and my friends stay away from me
because of my sickness. My family stands far away.

PSALM 38:10–11 NLV

King David could have had any woman he wanted. He was rich, handsome, and powerful. One day he saw a beautiful married woman named Bathsheba and decided he wanted her for his own. They slept together, and she became pregnant while her husband Uriah was out fighting in David's army. He tried to manipulate and cover up for his sin by inviting Uriah to come home and spend time with his wife. When Uriah refused, David ordered him to be on the front lines where he'd be killed. David's guilt over this situation made him physically ill. But even during this dark time, he knew God had not left him. No matter what we face, God never leaves us to face it alone.

131

DON'T GET DISTRACTED

"Be on your guard. Don't let the sharp edge of your expectation get dulled by parties and drinking and shopping."

LUKE 21:34 MSG

In this chapter in Luke, Jesus tells His disciples to be ready for His return. He was speaking not only to them, but to all of us. He shared signs we could look for to know the time is near. Though it's been 2,000 years since Jesus walked the earth, not much has changed about human nature. It's easy for us to get caught up with having fun in the moment and forget about eternity. He wants us to have joy while we're here, but the source of that joy should be the expectation that He's coming for us, and that while we wait, He'll do wonderful, exciting things in our lives. Don't get distracted by temporary fun and lose out on the greatest joy you'll ever know.

132

STOP IT NOW!

Make a clean break with all cutting, backbiting, profane talk. Be gentle with one another, sensitive. Forgive one another as quickly and thoroughly as God in Christ forgave you.

EPHESIANS 4:31–32 MSG

When Paul wrote letters to a specific church, he always addressed the issues that group was dealing with. Because human nature hasn't changed, their challenges are also our challenges. The people of the Ephesian church had a hard time getting along with one another. They squabbled and argued and said mean, cutting things to each other. Then they went around and gossiped about each other. They even used profanity. Paul told them to stop—to make a "clean break" with that behavior. We need to stop too. Those things have no place in a Christian's life. That kind of behavior only adds to our stress. Instead, be gentle, kind, and forgiving to everyone, just as Christ is with you. When we treat one another softly and with respect, they'll often start treating us the same way.

133

WAITING ON GOD

For I am waiting for you, O LORD.
You must answer for me, O Lord my God.
PSALM 38:15 NLT

David spent much of his life looking over his shoulder, wondering who was coming after him. He was a powerful man and could have put a stop to many of his problems. But he was also a wise man, and he didn't want to move in front of God. He knew that God's timing is perfect, and when we take things into our own hands instead of waiting on God, we often miss out on His best for us. Whether it's dealing with enemies, deciding who to date, or where to go to college, follow David's example. Step aside and wait on God to take care of things. Don't take one step or say one word until He gives you clear direction. He will always take care of those who trust Him, and He will never lead us down the wrong path.

134

DON'T GET EVEN

Don't hit back; discover beauty in everyone. If you've got it in you, get along with everybody. Don't insist on getting even; that's not for you to do. "I'll do the judging," says God. "I'll take care of it."

ROMANS 12:17–19 MSG

God doesn't want us to seek revenge on our enemies. If someone hits you with a fist or hurts you with their words, God wants us to let Him take care of it. That *doesn't* mean we can't defend ourselves. It *does* mean we're not supposed to try and get even. As much as possible, as far as it depends on us, we're supposed to try and live at peace with others. God sees everything, and He will do a much better job at delivering justice than we ever could. Try to be kind to everyone—especially those who are unkind to us. Pray for them. Stay away from them if you need to, but don't try to get revenge. That's God's responsibility.

135

WHEN YOU CAN'T SLEEP

I will lie down and sleep in peace.
O Lord, You alone keep me safe.
PSALM 4:8 NLV

It's interesting that David wrote these words. We know from his other writings that he often had trouble sleeping. When that happened, he spent time talking to God, pouring his heart out. Each time, he always came to the same conclusion: God is God. He is all-powerful. He is kind to His children, and He takes care of those who love Him. Once David talked through his anxiety, he remembered that he didn't have to worry. He didn't have to carry around all that fear. God, who never sleeps, is always watching over us, and He will keep us safe. Next time anxiety keeps you awake at night, follow David's example. Pour your heart out to God, and let His presence surround you. Sink into His love, knowing He will take care of you.

136

WALK AWAY FROM SIN

Walk away from the evil things in the world—
just leave them behind, and do what is right,
and always seek peace and pursue it.

1 PETER 3:11 VOICE

When we see things that aren't as they should be, we often get curious. We may be interested in what's happening and want to find out more about it. We may want to try it out for ourselves, to see what all the fuss is about. Or our motives may be more pure—we may think we can be a positive influence in a dark place. But God wants us to run away from evil, sinful things. We are His children and His representatives in this world. We have no business immersing ourselves in sin. When you witness things that are offensive to God, walk away. Always do what is right in His eyes and chase after the good things He's promised to those who love Him.

137

CHOOSE ONE OR THE OTHER

No one can serve two masters. If you try, you will wind up loving the first master and hating the second, or vice versa. People try to serve both God and money—but you can't. You must choose one or the other.

MATTHEW 6:24 VOICE

Can you imagine how you'd feel if you dated someone, only to learn they were dating someone else at the same time? Most of us would feel hurt and betrayed. When it comes to serious dating and marriage, we must choose one person. If we try to have that kind of loyalty to two people, it will never work. It cheapens the commitment. In the same way, we can't give our hearts to God and spend all our time and energy trying to make money or gain success or do something else without regard for what God wants. You have a choice about whom or what you'll pour your life into. Choose God.

138

BECAUSE OF WHAT HE DID

Now that we have been made right with God by putting our trust in Him, we have peace with Him. It is because of what our Lord Jesus Christ did for us.

ROMANS 5:1 NLV

If you ask people whether they're going to heaven when they die, many will answer "yes." But if you ask them why, a lot of them will say it's because they're a good person or because they've done more good than bad in their lives. They picture their actions being placed on a scale, and if the scale tips to the good, they're okay with God. The Bible teaches something different. We can't earn our way to heaven. We're all sinners—meaning we've all messed up and offended God at some point. The punishment for all sin is separation from God, or eternal death. But Christ took the punishment for us. Because of what Christ did for us, we've been made right with God.

139

FALLING IN LOVE

Those who love Your Law have great peace, and nothing will cause them to be hurt in their spirit.

PSALM 119:165 NLV

We're taught to read God's Word, pray, and trust God. It's possible to do those things in robot mode, without really feeling any excitement or passion. When we just go through the motions, we may wonder why we don't feel the peace God promised. This verse sheds some light on that question: "Those who love Your Law have great peace." The peace is a byproduct of loving God's Word, living it, and wanting to know more of it. The good news is, God's Word is addictive. The more we read it and study it and memorize it, the more we love it. It's okay to operate in robot mode if that's all you can do that day. God will bless your obedience. But ask God to change your heart. Ask Him to help you fall in love with His Word more each day.

140

THE AUTHOR OF PEACE

For God is not a God of disorder but of peace—
as in all the congregations of the Lord's people.
1 CORINTHIANS 14:33 NIV

Have you ever been in a situation where everything was in chaos? Maybe the teacher left the classroom for a few minutes and the students went wild. Or maybe you went to a shopping mall on the day after Thanksgiving and the crowds seemed out of control. That kind of environment gives us a sense of unease. We wouldn't describe those scenes as peaceful. In the early church (and in some churches today), the style of worship leaves people feeling more confused than peaceful. If you're ever in a situation that feels disjointed, remind yourself that God isn't the author of confusion. He's the author of peace. In every circumstance, make sure you're not adding to the chaos and confusion. As God's children, we should always try to bring peace.

141

THE SEED OF RIGHTEOUSNESS IS PEACE

The seed that flowers into righteousness will always be planted in peace by those who embrace peace.
JAMES 3:18 VOICE

The word *righteous* means free from guilt or sin. God is a righteous God. He is never motivated by evil or mean thoughts. He always does what is right, and He wants us to be like Him. But since we're human, our default mode is often selfish and sinful. If we want to be righteous, we must take steps to grow that kind of character. It doesn't happen overnight. But this verse tells us where to start. If we want to be righteous, like God, we must embrace peace. That means giving in instead of fighting, unless we're fighting for something that matters to God. It means letting others have their way about things that aren't morally wrong. Pursue peace whenever possible, and that will grow into righteousness.

142

FOOLISH OR WISE?

So be careful how you live. Don't live like fools, but like those who are wise.

EPHESIANS 5:15 NLT

According to *Dictionary.com*, a *fool* is a "silly or stupid person; a person who lacks judgment or sense." This verse contrasts a fool with those who are *wise*, who "have the power of discerning and judging properly as to what is true or right." Fools can look like they're having a lot of fun, because they laugh so much. They laugh at things that are good and moral and righteous, and they do the opposite. When we're surrounded by people making foolish choices, it's easy to get caught up in the moment and go along with the crowd. But their choices lead to regrets and painful consequences. Don't be fooled by the fools. Find the wisest, godliest people you know, and hang out with them. Act like them. You won't regret it.

143

HOW TO BECOME WISE

Get all the advice and instruction you can, so you will be wise the rest of your life.

PROVERBS 19:20 NLT

There's an old saying that goes, "Wise people learn from others' mistakes, smart people learn from their own mistakes, and fools never learn." God's Word often uses the words *foolish* and *pride* in the same context. Fools don't take instruction well, because they think they're always right. Their pride keeps them from becoming wise. If we want to learn and become wise, we must also be humble enough to recognize that we don't know everything. We all have much to learn about life. Whether it's taking instruction for an academic subject or understanding how to judge a person's character, seek out the wise people in your life and learn all you can from them. Wisdom comes from God. Ask Him to surround you with wise people.

144

LISTEN TO WISE PEOPLE

Fools think their own way is right,
but the wise listen to others.
PROVERBS 12:15 NLT

Have you ever known someone who just won't listen? Maybe that's even been said about you. Foolish people always think they're right, and they won't listen to what others have to say. This often leads them to make poor decisions that they regret. That happens to all of us at some point, but foolish people don't learn from their mistakes. Next time a difficult decision comes around, they do the same thing. They don't listen to the people who care about them. Instead, they do exactly what they want to do, even when others warn them against it. When faced with important decisions, seek out the wise people in your life and ask their advice. Then pray and ask the Holy Spirit, who is the true source of wisdom, to show you what to do.

145

DEALING WITH BULLIES

Do not repay evil with evil or insult with insult. On the contrary, repay evil with blessing, because to this you were called so that you may inherit a blessing.

1 PETER 3:9 NIV

We may think only the weak get pushed around by the bad guys. But even David, who was tall, strong, handsome, and successful, got bullied sometimes. If you're like David—a person who wants to please God and do what is right—others often see you as an easy target. *She won't fight back. She's a Christian.* The good news is that God sees it all, and He doesn't take kindly to people who mistreat His children. He will defend you. Just step back and let Him. He also made you strong and confident, so that you can stand up to your enemies when needed. Talk to God like David did. Pour out your heart to Him. He is right there, and He will never leave you to face your enemies alone.

146

WHEN I'M AFRAID

When I am afraid, I put my trust in you. In God, whose word I praise—in God I trust and am not afraid. What can mere mortals do to me?

Psalm 56:3–4 NIV

David was constantly looking over his shoulder. It seemed somebody was always coming after him at one point or another. Because he was human, he experienced the normal range of emotions, which included fear. It's not wrong to feel afraid. It is wrong, however, to huddle up and let the fear take over. David knew God well, and he knew he could cast that fear onto God. He knew he could trust God's character, which includes kindness, compassion, and love for His children.

Romans 10:17 says, "Faith comes from hearing the message, and the message is heard through the word about Christ." The more we know God, the easier it is to trust Him in difficult times.

147

I HAVE SEEN YOU

I have seen you in your sanctuary and gazed upon your power and glory.
PSALM 63:2 NLT

David wrote these words when his son Absalom was trying to take over the throne. David was forced to run and hide in the wilderness. He could have fought Absalom—he had a strong army to defend him—but he didn't *want* to risk killing his own son. Despite Absalom's actions, David loved his son. During this time, David and his men were forced to sleep wherever they could, in caves or behind rocks. They didn't always have enough to eat. But David recalled his time in worship, in the sanctuary. He recalled times when he felt God's presence so strong and thick, there was no question about God's power. Make worship a regular part of your routine. The more time you spend in God's presence, the more you can draw on those experiences during the dry spells of your life.

148

STEPS TO TAKE

"If my people, who are called by my name, will humble themselves and pray and seek my face and turn from their wicked ways, then I will hear from heaven, and I will forgive their sin and will heal their land."

2 CHRONICLES 7:14 NIV

Here, God tells us exactly what we need to do if we want to see results with our prayers. First, we must humble ourselves. That means we admit we're sinful and powerless to get out of any mess without God's help. We admit that God is our only hope. Next, we pray. We talk to God and tell Him everything, and we listen to Him as well. Third, we seek His face, which means we actively look for Him in all we do. Finally, we must say no to anything that doesn't please God. When we take these steps, God knows our hearts truly belong to Him. He loves to bless those who love Him with their whole selves.

149

GOD IS ROOTING FOR YOU

The Lord is for me, so I will have no fear.
What can mere people do to me? Yes,
the Lord is for me; he will help me. I will
look in triumph at those who hate me.

Psalm 118:6–7 NLT

This isn't the only time David reminded himself that with God on his side, no one could touch him. (See Psalm 56:4.) Hundreds of years later, Paul wrote similar words in Romans 8:31 (NIV): "If God is for us, who can be against us?" It's easy to get distracted by all the people and things that are against us. Maybe people are unkind and selfish. Maybe we're facing an unwanted illness, financial troubles, or a tough situation at home. But no matter what tries to hold us back, we can always know God is rooting for us. With God on our side, nothing else matters. Focus on Him and let the rest of it fade into the background.

150

LET HIM TAKE CARE OF IT

But no instrument forged against you will be allowed to hurt you, and no voice raised to condemn you will successfully prosecute you. It's that simple; this is how it will be for the servants of the Eternal; I will vindicate them.

ISAIAH 54:17 VOICE

God made this promise to His people—those who love Him with all their hearts. If someone makes plans to harm you, God won't allow it. That doesn't mean their plans won't ever begin. They may say things that hurt you. They may do awful things. But God is a God of justice. He will make sure evil is punished. Sometimes He will prevent bad things from happening. Other times we must trust that He's working for our good, even when we can't see it. He wants us to act wisely and stay away from danger when possible. He also wants us to trust Him to take care of things on our behalf.

151

RETURN TO GOD

Rend your heart and not your garments.
Return to the Lord *your God, for he is gracious and compassionate, slow to anger and abounding in love, and he relents from sending calamity.*

Joel 2:13 NIV

God told a prophet named Joel to urge the people of Judah to return to God. For a long time, they had lived however they wanted. They gave a nod to God's ways occasionally, but more out of tradition than from a sincere love. When they knew they'd sinned, they would tear (rend) their clothes to show God they were sorry. But they'd keep sinning, and nothing ever really changed. God wanted them to be sorry in their hearts. Joel urged the people to return to God, because He is loving and kind. If you're hesitant to go to God because of something in your past, remember that God is slow to anger. He loves you with all His heart.

152

WHEN WE LOOK UP

And when they looked up, Moses and Elijah were gone, and they saw only Jesus.
MATTHEW 17:8 NLT

Jesus needed a break from the crowds. He took Peter, James, and John with Him and went to a high mountain. While they were there, some amazing things happened. The three disciples watched as the prophets Moses and Elijah appeared and talked to Jesus. Then they heard a loud voice, and they realized it was God Himself. They immediately fell on their faces, because they knew they weren't worthy to see God. After a time, Jesus told them to get up, and they saw only Jesus there. Though we will probably never experience that, we can know there are things going on all around us in the spiritual world that we can't understand. But if we look up, we will always see Jesus' presence all around us. The rest of it isn't for us to know. All we need to concern ourselves with is loving Christ with all our hearts.

153

NO LONGER WILL I FEAR

No longer will I fear my tens of thousands of enemies who have surrounded me!

PSALM 3:6 VOICE

When David's son Absalom was trying to overthrow his father as king, he got thousands of people to support him. In fact, he tried to put together a 12,000-man army whose only job was to kill David. At that point in his life, David had lived through some pretty serious trials. He knew that if God was protecting him, nothing could harm him. The same is still true for us today. We can stay in God's protection by obeying Him and living our lives in a way that pleases Him. That doesn't mean nothing bad will ever happen. But as long as we make loving God and pleasing Him the most important goals of our lives, we can walk with confidence that He surrounds and protects us.

154

GOOD AND BEAUTIFUL THINGS

When your soul is famished and withering,
He fills you with good and beautiful things,
satisfying you as long as you live. He makes you
strong like an eagle, restoring your youth.
PSALM 103:5 VOICE

Anxiety and depression make most people tired. Even if our bodies aren't busy, our minds feel worn out. We question how much longer we can live this way. That's a good question, because that's not at all how God wants us to live. He wants to fill our lives with good and beautiful things. He wants us to experience joy that bubbles out of us while we're on this earth. He wants us to have peace and confidence and good relationships. We don't have to wait for heaven to experience His goodness. Push away sin. Run toward God and throw your whole self into His arms. Let Him fill you with His love, His kindness, His mercy, and all the beautiful things He has in store for your life.

155

MERCIFUL AND GRACIOUS

The Lord is compassionate and gracious, slow to anger, abounding in love. He will not always accuse, nor will he harbor his anger forever.

Psalm 103:8–9 NIV

Loving parents discipline their children. Without discipline, children grow up without the proper life skills to live positive, productive lives. But good parents don't make a punishment last forever. It only lasts long enough for the lesson to be learned. The goal should always be for the parent and child to return to a good, positive relationship as soon as possible. Though human parents don't always get this right, God does. His love is long and far-reaching. It takes a lot to make Him angry, because He is patient. When He does discipline us, it's because He wants the best for us. His desire is for us to get back into a close, loving relationship with Him as soon as possible. Do you need to return to Him today?

156

FROM EAST TO WEST

He has taken our sins from us as far as the east is from the west.

PSALM 103:12 NLV

Picture an imaginary line running across the universe from east to west. Technically, that line will never end. When King David wrote these words, he wrote from a place of gratitude. He'd committed some pretty big sins, and it would have been easy for him to get bogged down in guilt. He had more beautiful women than any man in the kingdom, yet he chose to commit adultery with the only wife of one of his loyal soldiers. When she became pregnant, David tried to cover up for it, eventually having the woman's husband killed. After his prophet confronted him, David felt ashamed. He told God he was sorry and asked for forgiveness. When we confess our sins and change our hearts, God marks them off the list. There's no need to feel guilty about something God has removed from our lives.

157

HE KNOWS ALL ABOUT US

He knows what we are made of.
He remembers that we are dust.
PSALM 103:14 NLV

Some people think they have to get their lives together before they approach God. They feel ashamed of who they are and what they've done, and they don't feel worthy of having a close relationship with Him. But God created us. He knows everything there is to know about us. He's not under any illusion that we're better than we are. He sees our flaws, our poor choices, and our bad attitudes and He loves us anyway. There's nothing we can do to remove His love from us. He knows we're small and our lives are temporary, but it doesn't matter to Him. He is madly and passionately in love with each of us, simply because He made us. Don't worry about your failures. Run to Him and rest in His deep love.

158

HOW TO BLESS GOD

Bless God, all creatures, wherever you are—
everything and everyone made by God.
PSALM 103:22 MSG

Most of us are familiar with the ways God blesses us. He gives us life, shelter, air to breathe, food to eat, and people to love. Those are just a few ways God shows His love for us. But this verse tells *us* to bless *God*. How do we do that? He already has everything He needs. What could we possibly give Him? The answer is simple—He wants our love. We can express that love in many ways: by doing His will, talking to Him, asking His advice, reading His Word, and loving other people. Anytime we do something that makes God smile, that makes Him proud to call us His children, we bless Him. And when we bless Him, He surrounds us with His presence, which blesses us as well.

159

I CAN'T, BUT GOD CAN

Each time he said, "My grace is all you need. My power works best in weakness." So now I am glad to boast about my weaknesses, so that the power of Christ can work through me.

2 CORINTHIANS 12:9 NLT

The world tells us we need to be strong. Capable. Smart. Talented. If we're not all those things, we can start to feel inadequate. But God tells us we don't have to be any of those things—at least not by ourselves. When we rely on our own strength and skills and abilities, we get the credit, and God gets left out. Instead of saying, "I can," God would rather hear us say, "I can't, but God can." He will often put us in situations that are just outside our comfort levels, forcing us to depend on Him. When that happens, we can smile and embrace the excitement of knowing God is about to do something big in our lives.

160

LIVING IN THESE TIMES

Be very careful, then, how you live—not as unwise but as wise, making the most of every opportunity, because the days are evil.

EPHESIANS 5:15–16 NIV

Paul wrote these words to the people living in Ephesus. This city was known for its pagan culture. They practiced many evil things, including prostitution and sexual sin as part of their religion. They lived in an "anything goes" culture where evil was celebrated and godliness was scoffed at. It sounds a lot like the world we live in today, doesn't it? It's popular to celebrate practices that go directly against God's Word. When we try to live godly, holy lives, people don't understand, and they often try to make us behave like them. Be wise. Ask God to help you see things the way He sees them. Make the most of every opportunity to please God and share His love. You might be the only Jesus someone else sees.

161

IT WILL BE OKAY

"I called out your name, O God, called from the bottom of the pit. You listened when I called out, 'Don't shut your ears! Get me out of here! Save me!' You came close when I called out. You said, 'It's going to be all right.'"

LAMENTATIONS 3:55–57 MSG

The book of Lamentations is a series of poems that lament, or mourn, the destruction of Jerusalem. The overall message of the book is that sin hurts us. It often has severe and painful consequences. Yet even in the middle of that pain—even when our circumstances are the result of our own poor choices—we can always go to God. He loves us. He doesn't like to see us hurting. He cares more about our souls than our circumstances, because He knows our circumstances are temporary. No matter what you're going through, call on God. Listen to Him whisper, "I love you. It will be okay."

162

DON'T BE AFRAID

Shortly before dawn Jesus went out to them, walking on the lake. When the disciples saw him walking on the lake, they were terrified. "It's a ghost," they said, and cried out in fear. But Jesus immediately said to them: "Take courage! It is I. Don't be afraid."

MATTHEW 14:25–27 NIV

In Roman culture, the night watch was divided into four sections so no one would have to lose a full night's sleep. The last watch was between 3 a.m. and 6 a.m. The disciples had been in the boat for hours and were around 3-4 miles from shore, according to John 6:19. When they saw a figure walking on water, they were terrified, as most of us would be. But Jesus reassured them. "It's me. Don't be afraid." Wherever you are, whatever your circumstances, Jesus wants to reassure you too. Look for Him—He's right there. Listen for His voice as He says, "It's me. Don't be afraid."

163

NEVER FAR AWAY

"The LORD your God is living among you. He is a mighty savior. He will take delight in you with gladness. With his love, he will calm all your fears. He will rejoice over you with joyful songs."

ZEPHANIAH 3:17 NLT

The prophet Zephaniah wrote these words thousands of years ago, but the message remains the same. God lives among us! When we accept His gift of salvation, His Holy Spirit makes His home right inside us, giving us courage, strength, and wisdom. God loves you so much. He delights in you. He's thrilled every time you seek Him out or talk to Him. Any time you feel anxious, He's right there, wrapping His arms around you, taking you by the hand, reminding you that it will be okay. He is so in love with you, He sings love songs over you. With that kind of support, we have no reason to ever feel alone or afraid.

164

PRINCIPLES FOR LIFE

Praise the Lord*. Blessed are those who fear the* Lord*, who find great delight in his commands. Their children will be mighty in the land; the generation of the upright will be blessed. Wealth and riches are in their houses, and their righteousness endures forever. Even in darkness light dawns for the upright, for those who are gracious and compassionate and righteous.*

Psalm 112:1–4 NIV

Some might take these verses out of context and say God promised to make His children rich and successful, but that misses the point. These verses hold principles to live by. Principles are fundamental truths. Living for God can help us avoid the pitfalls that sin brings. His wisdom helps us make wise choices, which lead to blessings. God promises to provide for our needs. Living for Him leads to a more fulfilling life here on earth. We can also take comfort in knowing we'll have all we could ever need in heaven.

165

HOW HE BLESSES THE RIGHTEOUS

Good will come to those who are generous and lend freely, who conduct their affairs with justice. Surely the righteous will never be shaken; they will be remembered forever. They will have no fear of bad news; their hearts are steadfast, trusting in the Lord. *Their hearts are secure, they will have no fear; in the end they will look in triumph on their foes.*

Psalm 112:5–8 NIV

God blesses everyone in a broad, general way. He gives us fresh air to breathe. He causes the earth to produce nourishing food for our bodies. We can all enjoy the beauty of a sunrise or the majesty of a starry night. But His blessings are more specific and personalized for those who follow Him, who make it a point to live righteous lives. When we're generous and kind because of our relationship with Him, we are blessed. He takes care of us, protects us, and gives us confidence because we choose to serve Him.

166

ALWAYS ON YOUR SIDE

David continued to address Solomon: "Take charge! Take heart! Don't be anxious or get discouraged. God, my God, is with you in this; he won't walk off and leave you in the lurch. He's at your side until every last detail is completed for conducting the worship of God."

1 CHRONICLES 28:20 MSG

Solomon was David's son. His mother was Bathsheba, the woman David committed adultery with. David had older sons, but he chose Solomon to be the next king because of his wisdom, and because God had told David that Solomon would be the one to build the temple. Solomon must have felt overwhelmed. He hadn't grown up thinking he'd be king one day. But David's words to his son can be applied to us today. Don't be anxious! God is with you. He will never, ever leave you. He will give you everything you need to do the things He has planned for you. He is always on your side.

167

DON'T BE AFRAID OF THEM

When you go forth to battle against your enemies and see horses and chariots and an army greater than your own, do not be afraid of them, for the Lord your God, Who brought you out of the land of Egypt, is with you.

DEUTERONOMY 20:1 AMPC

In this verse, Moses is talking to the Israelites. They're about to enter the Promised Land, and he won't go with them. He's offering some last words of wisdom before they part. Moses knows that although their new home will hold blessings, they'll also face troubles. The same is true today—each of our lives is filled with God's rich kindness and love, but we still face problems. Whether the problem is a person or a disease or a hard test or something else, we should remember these words. The trial may seem bigger than we are, but nothing is bigger than God. Don't be afraid. God fights for you, and His love for you never ends.

168

THE ANGEL OF THE LORD

The angel of the Lord encamps around those who fear him, and he delivers them.

PSALM 34:7 NIV

David reminds himself (and us) that the "angel of the Lord" is always nearby for those who fear Him. In this context, fear means deep respect and reverence, not a freaked-out terror. In the Old Testament, the angel of the Lord was Jesus Himself. For us, it's still Jesus, in the form of the Holy Spirit. He will never leave us, and He will always take care of us. He also has all the angels of heaven at His command. Though we can't see them, we can feel confident that they're doing whatever Jesus tells them, making sure those who love Him are taken care of. When you feel anxious and afraid, picture King Jesus and His mighty army surrounding you, holding you up and keeping you safe.

169

BRING IT ON

When evil people come to devour me, when my enemies and foes attack me, they will stumble and fall. Though a mighty army surrounds me, my heart will not be afraid. Even if I am attacked, I will remain confident.

PSALM 27:2–3 NLT

The final word of this verse sums up its message quite well. David was *confident* that God would take care of him. It wasn't just a nice thought. It wasn't a "close your eyes and wish for the best" kind of doubtful hope. It was almost a defiant kind of confidence—defiant to anyone who might dare threaten him. *Come on. Hit me with your best shot! See what happens. God won't let you hurt me.* That's the kind of faith God wants from each of us. When you face hard things or difficult people, pretend you're King David. Throw your shoulders back, lift your chin, look those problems in the eye, and wait to see how God carries you through.

170

THE BEST WAY

Teach me Your way, O Lord. Lead me in a straight path, because of those who fight against me.

PSALM 27:11 NLV

Here, David asks God to literally show him which way to go. He knew his enemies could be hiding around any corner, and he needed God's guidance to stay safe. If he had relied on his own skill and instinct, he might have been killed. Many other times, David prayed for God's wisdom. We can ask God for whatever we need, whenever we need it. Some people think they need to figure out the practical, earthly stuff on their own and only bother God with the spiritual stuff, but that's not true. Whether we need wisdom for how to respond in a relationship or we need literal directions because we took a wrong turn, we can ask God. He may not always guide us where we want to go, but He will always show us the best way.

171

HERE AND NOW

I would have been without hope if I had not believed that I would see the loving-kindness of the Lord in the land of the living. Wait for the Lord. Be strong. Let your heart be strong. Yes, wait for the Lord.

PSALM 27:13–14 NLV

Many people think they must wait until they're in heaven to receive good things from God. In their minds, their lives here on earth are just a series of hardships, and if they pass the tests, they get rewarded at the end. That's not true at all, and it's certainly not found in God's Word. God wants to bless us while we're here on earth. He loves us, and when you love someone, you want to do kind things for them. If you take a minute and think about things, you'll find countless ways God has already shown you His loving-kindness. The closer you stay to Him, the more you'll feel the effects of that overwhelming, joy-inspiring love.

172

IN HIS TIME

How long will they speak with arrogance?
How long will these evil people
boast? They crush your people, Lord,
hurting those you claim as your own.

Psalm 94:4–5 NLT

The writer of these verses asks God the same questions we all ask sometimes. Why do bad people get away with stuff? Why are they allowed to hurt the innocent and not get punished? These are valid questions, and there are no easy answers. We can be certain that God sees all. He hears all. And the guilty will be punished. It may not happen on our preferred timeline, but we can still move forward with confidence, knowing that when we love God, He will use every bad thing to create something good in our lives. Dealing with bullies can make us kinder and more compassionate. Struggling through illness can make us more resilient. Trust that God will deal with evil in His own way, in His own time. Right now, He is doing something beautiful in your life.

173

YESTERDAY, TODAY, AND FOREVER

Jesus Christ is the same yesterday and today and forever.
HEBREWS 13:8 NIV

If you were caught in a hurricane, what would you grab on to to stay safe? Would you cling to a tiny leaf on the ground? Of course not. You'd find something strong and stable, like a cement post. You'd want something that's not going to move, to help keep you anchored to the ground. Jesus Christ is our anchor in the storms of life. Life's winds may threaten to blow away our faith or destroy our peace. But those winds are like the big bad wolf in the classic "Three Little Pigs" story. They can't move something that has a strong foundation. Though people change, Christ does not. Our understanding of His truth may change, but His truth never will. When you face unsteady people or circumstances, let Him be your shelter. Hold onto Him, knowing His love, kindness, compassion, wisdom, and strength will never change.

174

A SEASON FOR EVERYTHING

For everything that happens in life—there is a season, a right time for everything under heaven.
ECCLESIASTES 3:1 VOICE

Most of us, if given the choice, would choose only good things. As for the bad things, the hardships, the negative people, the bullies, the struggles—we'd let those things roll right on by. But God, who loves us, knows what is best. He is working to make something beautiful and strong and useful in our lives. If we only ever eat candy, we'll end up with stomachaches and tooth decay. If we only ever hang out with our friends instead of doing schoolwork, we won't learn the skills we need to succeed in the future. God spaces things out for us into seasons of hardship and blessing so we don't stay overwhelmed. Whatever your season, thank Him! He's using it to do something amazing in your life.

175

BE A TRANSFORMER!

*Do not conform to the pattern of this world,
but be transformed by the renewing of your mind.
Then you will be able to test and approve what
God's will is—his good, pleasing and perfect will.*
ROMANS 12:2 NIV

Most of us have played with putty or playdough at some point. It's fun to place the dough into different molds to make hearts, stars, or even buildings. Because it's soft, dough will *conform* to the shape of whatever's around it. God doesn't want us to conform to the world around us. Instead, He wants to *transform* us into something totally different and more beautiful, like a caterpillar transforming into a butterfly. It's only through this transformation that we can show others what God wants to do in *their* lives. This amazing transformation happens by renewing our minds, a little at a time, by filling up our thoughts with His Word, praise, gratitude, and prayer. Are you conforming or transforming?

176

WE ARE LIKE SEEDS

This is the reason we do not give up.
Our human body is wearing out. But our
spirits are getting stronger every day.
2 CORINTHIANS 4:16 NLV

Have you ever studied the life cycle of a seed? A fully mature plant creates seeds. If a seed falls into the ground and is nurtured with the correct amounts of water and nutrients, it eventually splits open and a new plant is born. Our bodies are like those seeds. They house our spirits. If we nurture our spirits with the nourishment that comes only through a relationship with God, one day our bodies will die, but our spirits will be stronger than ever. Too often, we think of our lives here on earth as the end game, but nothing could be further from the truth. Right here, right now is only preparation for the joy we'll experience in eternity.

177

DON'T FOLLOW YOUR HEART

The little troubles we suffer now for a short time are making us ready for the great things God is going to give us forever. We do not look at the things that can be seen. We look at the things that cannot be seen. The things that can be seen will come to an end. But the things that cannot be seen will last forever.

2 CORINTHIANS 4:17–18 NLV

The world tells us to do what feels good and follow our hearts. But Jeremiah 17:9 tells us our hearts (emotions) are deceitful. If we use what feels good as our only guide, we will often end up on the wrong path. Consider your feelings but always weigh them against what God's Word says. If there's a conflict, follow God. He will never steer you wrong. The inconvenience of going against what feels right in the moment will fade away when we see all that God has in store for us.

178

NEVER STOP LEARNING ABOUT GOD

Wise men and women are always learning, always listening for fresh insights.

PROVERBS 18:15 MSG

Have you ever met someone who thinks they know it all? That person usually doesn't have a teachable spirit. They also do a lot more sharing their opinions than listening to others. God doesn't want us to be know-it-alls. Instead, He encourages us to always seek His wisdom. No matter how much wisdom He gives us, we'll never soak it all in. There's always more to learn about Him, His love, and His ways. God may or may not have called you to an academically challenging career that requires years of study. But He has definitely called each of us to study His Word, His character, and His way of doing things. Surround yourself with godly, wise people, and learn what you can. No matter how old you get, never stop seeking to know God more.

179

EVERY SINGLE PART

Every part of Scripture is God-breathed and useful one way or another—showing us truth, exposing our rebellion, correcting our mistakes, training us to live God's way. Through the Word we are put together and shaped up for the tasks God has for us.

2 TIMOTHY 3:16–17 MSG

Have you heard the term *cherry-picking*? It comes from the idea of a harvester choosing only the best, ripest fruit to put in their basket. While that might be a good practice for those trying to sell produce, we should never do that to God's Word. Those who cherry-pick the Bible choose only the scriptures they like and ignore the rest. This passage reminds us that every part of scripture is inspired by God, or God-breathed. Every verse is useful to show us His truth, convict us of sin, give us wisdom, and show us the right path to take.

180

HOPE IN JESUS

Jesus said, "Get up, take your bedroll, start walking." The man was healed on the spot. He picked up his bedroll and walked off.

JOHN 5:8–9 MSG

The earlier verses tell us this man had been lame for nearly 40 years. He stayed near the Pool of Bethesda. It was believed that when the waters stirred, it held healing properties. He wanted to be healed, but he couldn't walk, and he had no one to help him into the pool. Jesus asked the man if he wanted to get well, and the man explained his circumstances. Jesus had compassion on the man and healed him. Whatever your circumstances, whatever might be holding you back, you can know that God sees you too. He loves you, and He is full of compassion. Trust Him to heal your anxiety, your depression, or whatever else you are struggling with. It may happen immediately, but most likely, it will happen over time. Through Him, you have hope.

SCRIPTURE INDEX

OLD TESTAMENT

Proverbs

Ecclesiastes

Isaiah

NEW TESTAMENT

Hebrews

James

1 Peter

1 John

Revelation

GOT 5 MINUTES?

The 5-Minute Bible Study Map for Teen Girls

In just 5 minutes, you will Read (minutes 1–2), Understand (minute 3), Apply (minute 4), and Pray (minute 5) God's Word through interactive, visual Bible study maps. *The 5-Minute Bible Study Map for Teen Girls* includes more than 80 Bible studies that will speak to your heart in a powerful way.

Spiral Bound / 979-8-89151-186-6

Find This and More from Barbour Publishing at Your Favorite Bookstore or www.barbourbooks.com